NEHEMIAH

REBUILDING
A NATION

STAND
— on the —
WORD
Study Guide

NEHEMIAH

REBUILDING
A NATION

A 14-Day Journey through the Word
with Tony Perkins

FIDELIS PUBLISHING ®

ISBN: 9781956454468

Nehemiah: Rebuilding a Nation
A Stand on the Word Study Guide

© 2023 Tony Perkins

Content contributor: Dr. Kenyn Cureton
Cover design: Diana Lawrence
Interior layout design: Lisa Parnell
Copyeditor: Lisa Parnell

Order at www.faithfultext.com for a significant discount. Email info@fidelis publishing.com to inquire about bulk purchase discounts.

Fidelis Publishing, LLC Sterling, VA•Nashville, TN www.fidelispublishing.com

Manufactured in the United States of America

10 9 8 7 6 5 4 3 2 1

Contents

— DAY 1 —

Nehemiah: An Introduction

Welcome to the *Stand on the Word Study Guide* on *Nehemiah*. Nehemiah is one of my favorite books of the Bible. Although a short book, it is filled with history and practical applications for today. In fact, Nehemiah is a great book on leadership. On our fourteen-day journey through this book, we will find that Nehemiah shows us how to rebuild a nation. Yes, his initial mission was to motivate and mobilize his discouraged and demoralized people to rebuild the broken walls around Jerusalem. Yet before Nehemiah was finished, God used him to lead his shattered and scattered people to reconstitute into a unified nation, who returned to the Word of God, experienced revival, and renewed their covenant with the God of their forefathers. The book of Nehemiah provides a template for those of us who want to see a shattered and scattered America not only rebuild and unify but also return to the God of our Founders. But before we get into the first chapter, let's consider some background to the book of Nehemiah.

Background

The book of Nehemiah does not start out in the Holy Land. We find that Nehemiah was one of the Jewish exiles in the land of Persia, serving his king as the trusted cupbearer around the year 444

BC. Think of him as a top government security official. Meanwhile, the Jewish people who remained in and around Jerusalem were not only miserable but also vulnerable because the walls around Jerusalem were still in ruins. Consequently, they needed a leader to step forward. Enter Nehemiah. By the way, he had zero experience as a builder or a construction engineer. Yet God took this security official and molded him into an amazing leader who motivated and mobilized his people to press through danger and difficulty to accomplish their monumental mission. The book concludes around the year 430 BC with Nehemiah returning to serve as their godly governor, and Bible scholars believe the book was written shortly afterward either by Ezra the priest or by Nehemiah himself.

Now let's back up and set the book of Nehemiah in a broader historical timeline. The prophet Daniel was taken captive when Nebuchadnezzar took over Jerusalem in 605 BC. That was the first wave of captivity. A second was in 598 BC. And the third, which was considered to be the major captivity, took place when Jerusalem was destroyed in 586 BC.

The next major development was when Cyrus made the proclamation allowing the Jews to return and begin rebuilding the temple. That was in 538 BC. The first wave went back to Jerusalem under Zerubbabel, who became their governor, and the foundations of the second temple were laid in 537 BC. Then the construction stopped for about fifteen years.

The prophets Zachariah and Haggai encouraged the continuation of the rebuilding, which began in 520 BC, and then the second temple was finally completed in 515 BC. The focus returns to Persia with Esther, a Jew who became queen about 483 BC. Then the priest Ezra returned in 458 BC. This brings us to 444 BC when Nehemiah returned to Jerusalem to lead the effort to rebuild the walls.

So in total, from the time that Daniel was taken into captivity as a teen to when Nehemiah comes on the scene, roughly 160 years had transpired. Think about it. The walls of Jerusalem laid in ruins for more than 100 years. But under the godly and capable leadership of Nehemiah, the walls were rebuilt in less than two months.

How to Get the Most from the Study Guide

While the study guide offers spiritual insights and applications, the real impact comes from the words of Scripture, which is the Word of God. Please read the selected text for the day in your own Bible. God's Word is living and active (Heb. 4:12). The Spirit of God uses His Word to change your life. Nothing else can do that. So before reading the daily commentary, read God's Word! In fact, here are five habits to cultivate as you approach God's Word each day.

1. *Read it through:* Don't skip around. Read the entire selection of Scripture. If you are pressed for time, please read the Bible before you read the study guide notes. So read it through.
2. *Think it over:* Meditate on it. Let it marinate in your mind. If you can, take notes. We provide a notes page at the end of each day. Think it over.
3. *Pray it in:* Personalize the Scripture. Turn the verse that speaks to you into a prayer, and pray it into your life. Ask God what you need to do in response. That leads to the next habit.
4. *Live it out:* Consider ways to apply what God is revealing to you, ways you can obey Him. Put His word into practice. Make it a part of who you are, how you think, how you speak, and behave toward God and other people. In other words, take God's Word and live it out.
5. *Pass it on.* Don't keep it to yourself. People are in your life who need the same truth God has spoken to you in His Word. Share it. Pass it on.

About Stand on the Word

Stand on the Word is a ministry of Family Research Council, whose mission is to advance God's kingdom by championing faith, family, and freedom in public policy and the culture from a biblical worldview. The purpose of Stand on the Word is to lay the foundation for a biblical worldview through daily reading and application of God's Word. For the daily journey, we have created a chronologically prioritized reading plan through the entire Bible that can be accessed at frc.org/Bible or simply by texting the word *Bible* to 67742.

— DAY 2 —
Today's Reading: Nehemiah 1

Verse of the Day

So it was, when I heard these words, that I sat down and wept, and mourned for many days; I was fasting and praying before the God of heaven.

Nehemiah 1:4

Please read the entire Scripture selection in your own Bible and highlight or underline verses that stand out to you before you read the observations and engage the questions below.

Let's begin in Nehemiah 1:1, "The words of Nehemiah the son of Hachaliah." Skip down to verse 11 for more info about this man: "For I was the king's cupbearer." The king mentioned here is the ruler of Persia, which at that time was the world's most powerful empire. Most Bible scholars believe this was Artaxerxes I who ruled from 465–424 BC. As cupbearer, Nehemiah was in a prominent role. Today, we would see him as the equivalent to a secret service agent with top government security clearance, protecting the world's most powerful leader. Sometimes assassins tried to take out a king by putting poison in his drink or his food, and it was the cupbearer's job to taste test everything to make sure it was safe. In that day, assassination attempts were not uncommon. The books of Kings and Chronicles include some palace intrigue, even some murders of the kings of Israel and Judah. It was no different in foreign nations. For example, Daniel served eight different foreign leaders. Some of those disappeared quickly and not by natural causes. Needless to say, Nehemiah, as cupbearer of the king, was in a trusted position.

His was also in a position of incredible potential influence because of the amount of "face time" Nehemiah had with the powerful king. Here was this Jewish captive in a heathen nation, and yet he had influence. This has implications for us today. We can be serving in an ungodly environment and surrounded by godless people, and yet we can be salt and light; we will influence those around us provided we are trustworthy and perform our duties with excellence. As we read later, Nehemiah indeed had a great deal of influence.

Now let's look at the rest of verse 1 and verses 2–3: "It came to pass in the month of Chislev, *in* the twentieth year, as I was in Shushan the citadel, that Hanani one of my brethren came with men from Judah; and I asked them concerning the Jews who had escaped, who had survived the captivity, and concerning Jerusalem. And they said to me, 'The survivors who are left from the captivity in the province *are* there in great distress and reproach. The wall of Jerusalem *is* also broken down, and its gates are burned with fire.'" So, Nehemiah got this report of what the situation was like back in Jerusalem, and it was not what he wanted to hear!

It was about a four-month journey between Shushan in Persia, where they were, to Jerusalem. They didn't have CNN or any other news outlet with their cameras constantly streaming live footage from a remote location. Probably was a good thing. News had to travel by a person who went back and forth, usually on a horse or camel, sometimes on foot. When Nehemiah heard the report of how bad things really were in Jerusalem, it went straight to his heart. He was overwhelmed with concern and compassion for his people back in the Promised Land. Not surprisingly, verse 4 says, "So it was, when I heard these words, that I sat down and wept, and mourned *for many* days; I was fasting and praying before the God of heaven."

Let us zoom in on this prayer of Nehemiah. In this troubling situation of his, Nehemiah immediately prayed. We can focus on four elements of this prayer, and if we apply them to our own prayer lives, they will be enriched.

First, let us look at the *purpose* of his prayer. Was he praying for himself? No. He had everything he needed. Nehemiah was well taken care of as the cupbearer to the king. But he felt the burden of his suffering people, and he began to intercede for them. Oh, how much more of this kind of selfless intercession is needed in our nation and in our churches today! We are truly living in the "me" generation. It is time, Christian, to start falling on your knees, and when you do, pray for others.

Second, we see the *posture* of his prayer. Now by posture, I am not necessarily talking about physical posture, although that is important. I am talking about a condition of the heart. Whether we're on our face or standing or we're sitting down, our most effective prayer is when we are desperate for God. Nehemiah was desperate and had no other place to go. He was burdened for his people, and he knew the only answer was to seek the King of kings and the Lord of lords. When you and I are desperate, then we'll begin to hear from God. Nehemiah was humbling himself before God. When we begin to live totally and absolutely dependent upon God, that's when we begin to hear from and see God working in our lives.

Fasting is a way we humble ourselves before God. Few things remind us of our human frailty and dependence upon God more than hunger. But more importantly, it's also a visible display of us placing God as our priority and our spiritual need over our most basic physical need. When you or I say, "You know what, I'm going to fast during this mealtime," or "I'm going to fast for this day," or "I'm going to engage in this form of denying myself food so that I can focus on God in prayer and reading of Scripture," what we are doing is reordering our priorities and saying our spiritual health is more important than our physical needs and desires. And God sees that. We are humbling ourselves.

Third, we see the *pattern* of Nehemiah's prayer in verses 5–6. Notice in verse 5 how he praised the character and appealed to the mercy of God: "And I said: 'I pray, LORD God of heaven, O great and awesome God, *You* who keep *Your* covenant and mercy with those who love You and observe Your commandments.'" Appealing to God's character and seeking to defend that character is a key to effective prayer. Nehemiah started out his whole prayer not by immediately going to the problem but by reminding God (not that God needs to be reminded) of His character.

Next, notice in verse 6 how Nehemiah pleaded with God: "please let Your ear be attentive and Your eyes open, that You may hear the prayer of Your servant which I pray before You now, day and night, for the children of Israel Your servants." This is the posture of humility at work that we referred to earlier. Nehemiah then was more specific in his request: "and confess the sins of the children of Israel which we have sinned against You. Both my father's house and I have sinned." We must confess our sins. Unrepentant sin in our lives will keep us from having the fellowship with God that He wants us to have with Him and we hunger for. This goes beyond our lives before Him as individuals to the life of our nation. Our sin is prominent in this nation. But it's not just the nation. It's in our communities. It's in our own homes. It's in our own lives.

Notice what Nehemiah did not do. He didn't point fingers. He didn't stand detached from the Jewish people. Rather he acknowledged and took ownership of where the nation was and how they had disobeyed God. See, in order to bring about change, we must take ownership. And here he took ownership. He confessed the sin of the people—the children of Israel—but he included himself. He identified with the sin of the people. If you and I are serious about seeking the face of God, we must turn from our wicked ways. We must confess our sins; we must take ownership of what we've done. And here's the good news: as soon as we do that, God is ready and willing to forgive and wipe the record clean (see 1 John 1:9).

Then notice in the pattern of his prayer that Nehemiah not only confessed the sins of the people, including his own, but also he prayed the Word of God. Look at verses 8–9: "'Remember, I pray, the word that You commanded Your servant Moses, saying, "*If* you are unfaithful, I will scatter you among the nations; but *if* you return to Me, and keep My commandments and do them, though some of you were cast out to the farthest part of the heavens, *yet* I will gather them from there, and bring them to the place which I have chosen as a dwelling for My name." We see that he actually prayed back Scriptures from Deuteronomy (see 4:27; 30:1–5). By the way, it is an effective way to pray. To take God's Word and pray it back to Him.

Fourth and finally, we see in verse 10 the *petition* of his prayer: "Now these *are* Your servants and Your people, whom You have redeemed by Your great power, and by Your strong hand. O LORD, I pray, please let Your ear be attentive to the prayer of Your servant, and to the prayer of Your servants who desire to fear Your name; and let Your servant prosper this day, I pray, and grant him mercy in the sight of this man." Nehemiah heard of the devastation of the city and the distress of the people, and he was moved with compassion and concern so much that he fasted and he prayed that God would present a solution and heal their land. So, he made his petition.

Well, Nehemiah followed God's prescription—humbling himself with fasting, seeking the face of God with prayer, confessing sin in genuine repentance (see 2 Chron. 7:14). And during the course of this period of time, which was about four months, God tapped Nehemiah on the shoulder, spoke to him in his Spirit, and He said, "I've heard your prayer, Nehemiah. Now, I want you to be a part of the solution." So at the end of this chapter, we see Nehemiah's "Here am I, send me" moment. I want to warn you here. If you're genuine and true and authentic in seeking His face and desiring to see the spiritual walls rebuilt around your families, your children, your grandchildren, your communities, your country, then do not be surprised if, during the course of it, God taps you on the shoulder and says, "I've heard your prayer. I've heard your prayer because you're praying My will. It is My desire for the spiritual walls to be rebuilt. But I want you to be a part of rebuilding them." You must have the same "Here am I, send me" moment that Nehemiah had.

The big takeaway from this chapter is, Nehemiah was a man of prayer. Most of this first chapter (vv. 4–11) contains his prayer. He wasn't like most of us who get on social media and rant. He didn't complain about the plight of the Jews and his brothers and sisters back in Jerusalem. He got on his face before God. His focus on prayer, however, continues throughout the entire book of Nehemiah. You see, this was not just a one-time, drive-by prayer; it was a way of life for Nehemiah. I think there's something we can learn from that. This was someone who was used in such a profound way to alter the course of a nation, and he was so focused on prayer. Nehemiah was a man who arose to meet the great overwhelming need around him first through prayer. And as a result, he altered the course of a nation.

I think we would do well to spend more time in prayer than venting on social media platforms. There's a place to communicate, but if we're looking for solutions, and we want to be a part of solving problems, we need to become people of prayer. Look around. What great need captures your heart? Take it to God in prayer. He may tap you to be a part of the solution.

Questions for Reflection and Discussion

1. What was Nehemiah's response to his brother Hanani's report of the sad situation of the broken-down walls back in Jerusalem?
   a. He wept and mourned for days.
   b. He fasted and prayed before God for months.
   c. He made a bold request of the Persian king to lead a rebuilding effort.
   d. All of the above.

2. What position of responsibility did Nehemiah have in the kingdom, and why was that important?

Notes on Today's Bible Reading

_____

_____

_____

_____

_____

_____

_____

_____

_____

_____

_____

— DAY 3 —

Today's Reading: Nehemiah 2

Verse of the Day

> And I told them of the hand of my God which had been
> good upon me, and also of the king's words that he had
> spoken to me. So they said, "Let us rise up and build." Then
> they set their hands to this good work.
>
> *Nehemiah 2:18*

Please read the entire Scripture selection in your own Bible and highlight
or underline verses that stand out to you before you read the observations
and engage the questions below.

In this chapter, Nehemiah goes before King Artaxerxes. Look at
verse 1: "And it came to pass in the month of Nisan, in the twentieth year of King Artaxerxes, when wine was before him, that I
took the wine and gave it to the king." Note that the period of time
that transpired between chapter 1 and chapter 2 was about four
months. Consequently, for four months, Nehemiah had been praying, fasting, and based upon his ready answer in verse 6, even planning for the opportunity that God might give him something to do.

The moment of opportunity he had been praying for came. He
was in the presence of the king, a place where few people had the
opportunity to be. Now he did not have the privilege of bringing

up issues before the king unless the king inquired of him. So Nehemiah went before Artaxerxes, and the king saw that his countenance was falling—he was sad. And that's not a good thing. To keep one's head, literally, it was wise to be happy and cheerful in the presence of the king. Yet Nehemiah's heart was greatly burdened for his people.

So, let's see what occurs in verses 2–4: "Therefore the king said to me, 'Why *is* your face sad, since you *are* not sick? This *is* nothing but sorrow of heart.' So I became dreadfully afraid, and said to the king, 'May the king live forever! Why should my face not be sad, when the city, the place of my fathers' tombs, *lies* waste, and its gates are burned with fire?' Then the king said to me, 'What do you request?' So I prayed to the God of heaven."

There it is again: he prayed. But he didn't only pray. He told the king the problem. The king asked him, "Well, what do you request?" Think about it. What if Nehemiah replied, "I don't know. I just wanted to bring you a problem. Over in Jerusalem, the walls are torn down, and the gates are burned with fire, and my people are discouraged and depressed. I just thought I'd tell you the problem." As the leader of a ministry, I often tell employees, "If you bring me a problem, bring me a solution." And that is exactly what Nehemiah did.

Now, from this passage, we discover five characteristics that prepared Nehemiah for this moment of opportunity to serve, and these principles of preparation that worked for Nehemiah apply to our lives as well. The first characteristic we see in the life of Nehemiah is his dependence upon God: "Then the king said to me, 'What do you request?' So I prayed to the God of heaven" (2:4). He'd been praying for four months. We may think he was prayed out; but instead, he was prayed up, and it became a way of life for him. He was serious about his prayer. He was committed to it. He was unyielding in his determination to get an answer from God.

Remember, we can do all that we can on our end, and then some, to be prepared, but we must depend upon God ultimately for success. And we read this over in Proverbs 21:31: "The horse is prepared against the day of battle, but deliverance is of the LORD." So prayer is evidence of our dependence upon God. Proverbs 3:5–6 says, "Trust in the LORD with all your heart, and lean not on your own understanding; in all your ways acknowledge Him, and He shall direct your paths." One of the characteristics of someone who is preparing himself to be used by God is someone dependent upon God. Nehemiah's heart was burdened to the point of praying and fasting for four months. See, the greater the desperation, the greater the declaration of our dependence upon God. And here, Nehemiah continued to pray, anticipating that God would move, and looked for the moment when God would open the door.

Second, not only was there this dependence upon God, but there was a dedication in conduct. In verse 5, the king opens the door for Nehemiah, and this is the moment he had been waiting for. And he said, ". . . if your servant has found favor in your sight." You see, the opportunities before us are connected to our behavior in the past. Often we're looking for God to use us, yet we may be neglecting the very present responsibility we have. Some are like the guy in the parable of the talents, who hid his money instead of investing it. We cannot expect God to use us unless we're dedicated to the duty He has called us to even now.

You and I must be diligent and faithful; we must be dedicated in our conduct now, understanding that our future opportunities depend upon dedication to our present duties. Proverbs 22:29 says, "Do you see a man who excels in his work? He will stand before kings; He will not stand before unknown men." It was because of Nehemiah's track record of dedicated conduct, his devotion to his responsibilities, and his excellence at his work that he had favor with the king.

Think about this for a moment. What kind of favor do you have with King Jesus. Have you been faithful in what He has given you to do? God is looking for those who are faithful and devoted in their conduct to what He has called them to do before He entrusts them with greater opportunity to serve Him. So Nehemiah depended on God and was dedicated in his conduct, and we should be too.

Third, Nehemiah was diligent in his planning. Look at verse 6: "Then the king said to me (the queen also sitting beside him), 'How long will your journey be? And when will you return?' So it pleased the king to send me; and I set him a time." Nehemiah had thought through this. He had been diligent in planning out all the details. The journey from the Persian capital there to Jerusalem was nine hundred miles, which would take him two months. And once he got there with all the needed materials, he had to mobilize the people to rebuild the walls and the gates.

Let's consider all the unknowns Nehemiah had to deal with because he was a security official, not a builder or construction engineer. There were a lot of moving parts; but for four months, he was praying to God. And God, through the Holy Spirit, was likely giving him the answers piece by piece. That must be the case because when he was asked, "How long will you be gone?" Nehemiah immediately gave the king an answer and set a time. But he didn't stop there.

The fourth principle is that Nehemiah was devoted to detail. He not only said, "Well, I need to go back because I have walls to build, I've got to build some other structures, and I am going to need building materials." He gets quite specific. Look at verses 7–8: "Furthermore I said to the king, 'If it pleases the king, let letters be given to me for the governors of the region beyond the River, that they must permit me to pass through till I come to Judah, and a letter to Asaph the keeper of the king's forest, that he must give me timber to make beams for the gates of the citadel which pertains to the temple, for the city wall, and for the house that I will occupy.'" He asked for letters not only to the keeper of the forest to get the wood, but he realized he was going to run into some political resistance. So he asked for letters from the king to these governors. If they tried to stop him—asking, "Who gave you the right to come through here?"—he would produce a letter. See Nehemiah paid close attention to, he cared about, the details. And let me tell you someone else who cares even more about the details. God cares about the details. Remember over in Genesis 6 when He told Noah to build the ark, or look at Exodus 25 when He told Moses to build the tabernacle. In fact, it takes an entire five chapters for God to give Moses the specifics. God is concerned with the details. Nehemiah was devoted to the details, and we should be too.

The final principle of preparation is that Nehemiah was discrete in conversation. Look at verses 11–12: "So I came to Jerusalem and was there three days. Then I arose in the night, I and a few men with me; I told no one what my God had put in my heart to do at Jerusalem . . . ." He didn't know who would be with him and who might be against him when he showed up there in Jerusalem. Think about it for a moment: This guy had a pretty easy life being the cup-bearer to the king, and all of a sudden he showed up and the people said, "Who is this guy? What does he know? He hasn't been here." And so, Nehemiah wanted to be very careful in how he approached the people. He knew he could encounter the cold-water committee, ready to extinguish the passion to rebuild. Therefore, he needed all the facts, so he could turn back the naysayers.

We need to learn that lesson from Nehemiah. We don't need to go out half cocked, letting our passion pre-empt our preparation because not everyone has heard the same thing that we've heard. And if we go off and tell the first person we encounter, "Well, God just told me this and I'm ready to do this," he might say, "God didn't tell me that, so why should I listen to you?" and you don't have an answer. Nehemiah wasn't going to let that happen.

Nehemiah did all his preparation in Persia, but remember, Nehemiah had not been to Jerusalem. All he had was secondhand information. He prayed, and God spoke to him, but he needed to have firsthand knowledge and understanding. And so, he spent three days there. He went out at night with only his core group, but he didn't tell the local leaders there what he was going to do. He explored, and he saw firsthand how great the need was. And in fact, I'm sure he probably went back and changed some of his calculations, moved some of his plans around based upon that firsthand information, and then he went and laid out the plan. Again, we've got to be discreet in sharing what God has told us because not everyone will be with us. But we also must be prepared to defend what God has given us by having a greater understanding of what the need really is. Nehemiah was prepared.

Now Nehemiah is ready to make his case and notice what happens in verses 17–18: "Then I said to them, 'You see the distress that we *are* in, how Jerusalem *lies* waste, and its gates are burned with fire. Come and let us build the wall of Jerusalem, that we may no longer be a reproach.' And I told them of the hand of my God which had been good upon me, and also of the king's words that he had spoken to me. So they said, 'Let us rise up and build.' Then they set their hands to *this* good *work*." Nehemiah had their buy-in, and they were ready to join him in rebuilding the walls. "This good work" was Nehemiah's purpose. He was a man of prayer. He was a man who planned and prepared. But he was also a man of purpose. And I think we need to live with a greater sense of purpose. Each of us, if we are believers in Jesus Christ and have been saved, have a purpose. We have been given a mission, and we need to be focused on that purpose and where God has planted us.

Then we see also that Nehemiah was a man of persistence. As soon as he had begun the work, the critics showed up. Look at verse 19: "But when Sanballat the Horonite, Tobiah the Ammonite official, and Geshem the Arab heard *of it*, they laughed at us and despised us, and said, 'What *is* this thing that you are doing? Will you rebel against the king?'" Now remember, opposition wasn't a new thing. Zerubbabel the governor faced it back in the days of the prophets Haggai and Zachariah. Opposition was part of the reasons the rebuilding of the temple stalled for fifteen years. Here it was again. Look at Nehemiah's response in verse 20: "So I answered them, and said to them, 'The God of heaven Himself will prosper us; therefore we His servants will arise and build, but you have no heritage or right or memorial in Jerusalem.'" Here we see Nehemiah showing persistence, following his purpose, and pursuing his plans based upon his prayer. We need to be like Nehemiah, praying to God for the opportunity to solve the problems that surround us, and being prepared to seize those opportunities when they are handed to us.

Questions for Reflection and Discussion

1. How did the people respond to Nehemiah's challenge to rebuild the walls, which had the backing of the Persian king and was marked by the providential hand of God?

2. How did Sanballat, Tobiah, and Geshem respond to the news that Nehemiah was leading an effort to rebuild the walls around Jerusalem?
    a. Laughed at them
    b. Despised them
    c. Charged them with rebellion
    d. All of the above

Notes on Today's Bible Reading

— DAY 4 —

Today's Reading: Nehemiah 3

Verse of the Day

> After him Benjamin and Hasshub made repairs opposite their house. After them Azariah the son of Maaseiah, the son of Ananiah, made repairs by his house.
>
> *Nehemiah 3:23*

Please read the entire Scripture selection in your own Bible and highlight or underline verses that stand out to you before you read the observations and engage the questions below.

We ended our study of chapter 2 with Nehemiah challenging the people of Jerusalem to arise and participate in rebuilding the walls. In the face of ridicule and false charges of rebellion against the king of Persia from Sanballat the Horonite, Tobiah the Ammonite official, and Geshem the Arab, Nehemiah replied, "The God of heaven Himself will prosper us; therefore we His servants will arise and build, but you have no heritage or right or memorial in Jerusalem" (v. 20). You've got to love this guy. Nehemiah is on a mission from God, and nothing and no one will deter him!

In chapter 3, we read the names of all the unsung heroes who participated in the rebuilding of the walls. Why did God see to it that all of their names appear in Scripture? I believe it was to honor them. They were a part of building a legacy. On one of my trips to

Israel, I actually saw what is believed to be part of the wall around Jerusalem that Nehemiah built nearly twenty-five hundred years ago. By arising and participating, they made a lasting difference. So the truth from our study is that Nehemiah led the people to not only build a wall but build a legacy. They changed their nation's future by arising from their discouragement and despair to confront the problem before them. They embraced God's prescription, which required their participation. So there are three movements I want us to dissect from chapter 3: the problem, the prescription, and the participation.

First, let's consider the problem. While God's judgment of seventy years of captivity had ended more than eighty years before, His people were still living in the effects of the reproach of their sin as a nation. When Nehemiah told them in 2:17 that the walls were torn down and the gates were burned with fire, honestly, he didn't tell them anything they didn't know. Most of them had been stepping over and around the debris all their lives. Some of them had never known anything else. Consequently, they were discouraged and living in almost a constant state of despair. Because the walls were torn down, they were regularly harassed and they lived in fear of their enemies. You see, the walls represent safety and security and identity. Now I'm talking about building walls—not the kind needed on our southern border; I'll leave that one to someone else. I'm talking about the spiritual walls around our families, around our communities, around our nation. When those walls are torn down, we're open to attacks from our enemies. So obviously, Jerusalem's walls being down was a big problem.

Nehemiah arrived, he spent three days praying and assessing the situation firsthand, and then he presented the problem. However, second, he didn't only present the problem, but he proposed a prescription, a solution. I'm sure you've experienced people in your life who brought you only the problem. Can you imagine what would have happened if Nehemiah came from Persia, looked over the situation, and just *told* them the problem? If Nehemiah had only said, "Hey folks, you have a big problem. The walls are torn down, and the gates are burned with fire." They might have run him out of town. They knew they had a problem. What they needed was a solution.

I can tell you, as one who has employed a number of people and have people working for me now, that dog won't hunt. I tell them, "If you bring me a problem, bring me a solution." Well, that is exactly what Nehemiah did. Remember what he said in 2:17–18: "'Come and let us build the wall of Jerusalem, that we may no longer be a reproach. And I told them of the hand of my God which had been good upon me, and also of the king's words that he had spoken to me. So they said, 'Let us rise up and build.' Then they set their hands to this good work." Apply this principle to the spiritual walls being torn down in America. The prescription, or the solution, is to rebuild the spiritual walls so that others might experience the abundant life Jesus gave His life for us to enjoy.

Third, look at what the people did. They participated. Everyone did. We read about the participation of the priests in verse 1. There were also the goldsmiths and the perfumers in verse 8. I'll bet they smelled good. There were also rulers (v. 9) and the women (v. 12) who worked on the walls. God is an equal opportunity employer. The Levites were a part of the rebuild (v. 17), as were the merchants (v. 32). There was only one group, the Tekoites, who were known as the nobility or upper crust, who didn't put their shoulder to the work of the Lord (v. 5). But fortunately, we read later in the chapter that the actual people of Tekoa worked harder to make up for that one elitist group (v. 27). But the people, nearly everyone, participated in rebuilding the walls.

What is the message? There is room for every one of you on the wall God wants to build around your family, around your communities, and around your nation. It doesn't matter how old you are. It doesn't matter how young you are. It doesn't matter whether you're male or female. It doesn't matter if you're rich or poor. God has a place for you in his plan.

Listen, we will not see the spiritual walls of our nation rebuilt if we only leave it to the professionals. If we leave it to the politicians, even the Christian ones, or if we leave it to the ministers or to our Christian school educators or Sunday school teachers, the work will not be as successful as it could be. Folks, it will not happen unless every one of us takes our place on the wall, rebuilding from the rubble and ruins that have resulted from the constant attacks we have seen in this nation. That was the strategy. This was no group of professional builders—just everyday people like you and me.

But there is more here for us in chapter 3. This is one of the most fascinating passages of Scripture for me in terms of God's strategy. Notice where most of them worked. Look at verse 10: "Next to them Jedaiah the son of Harumaph made repairs *in front of his house*. And next to him Hattush the son of Hashabniah made repairs." Now look at verse 23: "After him Benjamin and Hasshub made repairs *opposite their house*. After them Azariah the son of Maaseiah, the son of Ananiah, made repairs *by his house*." Skip down to verses 28–29: "Beyond the Horse Gate the priests made repairs, each *in front of his own house*. After them Zadok the son of Immer made repairs *in front of his own house*." They each worked in front of or near their own homes, where they had the most at stake.

I can imagine the conversation going something like this:

"Here's the plan; we're all going to rebuild this wall."

"OK, we're in."

"Now, do you want somebody else building the wall around your house, or do you want to build it?"

"Oh no. I want to build the wall next to my house."

I can tell you what I would be saying: "I'm going to build it myself, and I'm going to build it extra high and double thick. I want to make sure that wall stands." So, this is a brilliant strategy. Nehemiah let's each of them build the walls around their houses. For those who were living outside of Jerusalem, they built the walls nearest them and in their neighborhood. Everyone had something at stake.

You say, well, what does that mean to me? Here it is. You want to rebuild the spiritual walls of America? Start closest to you and nearest your heart. Start in your home. Start by rebuilding the spiritual walls around your home. What influences are flowing into your home via social media, cable, or the internet that are breaching the walls and robbing your family? Put a stop to it. What about the education of your children? Are you talking to your children about what they're learning in school? Do you participate in school-board meetings? Be vigilant.

What about their spiritual development? It is not primarily the job of ministers and teachers to teach your children the truth of God's Word; it is up to you. Be proactive. Each time you pray with your children, your grandchildren, each time you study Scripture with them, you're putting another brick on the wall. You're fortifying them, you're securing them, and you're building a legacy for them.

Do you want to leave a legacy? Something you're remembered for? Something that will last beyond your life and literally speak into eternity? Begin rebuilding the spiritual walls around your home. And if enough of us will do that, we will see the rebuilding of our communities. And if enough communities will rebuild their spiritual walls, by the grace of God we may just see the spiritual walls rebuilt all over America. We must seize this moment, this opportunity, just as Nehemiah did when he had favor from the king to rebuild the walls of Jerusalem. May we rise up and build the spiritual walls of America that God might bless this country again.

Questions for Reflection and Discussion

1. What was the strategic benefit of having people build the part of the wall in front of their own house?

2. What were some of the diverse groups who were building the wall?
   a. Priests and Levites
   b. Goldsmiths and perfumers
   c. Nobles and foreigners
   d. Women and merchants
   e. All of the above

Notes on Today's Bible Reading

_____

_____

_____

_____

_____

_____

_____

_____

_____

_____

Nehemiah: Rebuilding a Nation

_____

_____

_____

_____

_____

_____

_____

_____

_____

_____

_____

_____

_____

_____

_____

_____

_____

_____

_____

— DAY 5 —
Today's Reading: Nehemiah 4

Verse of the Day

And I looked, and arose and said to the nobles, to the leaders, and to the rest of the people, "Do not be afraid of them. Remember the Lord, great and awesome, and fight for your brethren, your sons, your daughters, your wives, and your houses."

Nehemiah 4:14

Please read the entire Scripture selection in your own Bible and highlight or underline verses that stand out to you before you read the observations and engage the questions below.

Today, we are studying Nehemiah 4, and we find the work of rebuilding the wall faces opposition. Not that surprising, is it? Here is a saying proven over the years: When God calls, and we arise and obey, expect the enemy to arise and oppose. But we must remember the greatness of our God and the importance of our cause. And then we must persist. We also need to understand this: the authentic Christian life is not a picnic; rather, it's a battle—not a physical battle but a spiritual one.

Paul wrote this in Ephesians 6:12: "For we do not wrestle against flesh and blood, but against principalities, against powers, against the rulers of the darkness of this age, against spiritual hosts of wickedness in the heavenly places." The word *fight* appears 102 times in the New King James Version of the Bible. *Battle* is found nearly 200 times. The Lord Jesus calls us to count the costs of following Him and puts it in terms of warfare, telling a parable about a king wanting to go to war, calculating whether his force can take the enemy. Jesus called His followers with this sobering message in Luke 9:23: "If anyone desires to come after Me, let him deny himself, and take up his cross daily, and follow Me." To follow Jesus Christ means we must count the cost and deny ourselves what we want, what we desire, and even our own reputation. We must lay all that down, take up a cross, and follow Him.

So we see in this passage, as soon as the construction of the wall began, it was like a trigger. It's like when the lights go out in a cheap hotel and the cockroaches begin their work. Here we see the opposition scurrying forth to try and impede the work of God with various tactics. But Nehemiah met each threat with prayer and preparation. He was armed for the battle.

Look at Nehemiah 4:1–9.

"But it so happened, when Sanballat heard that we were rebuilding the wall, that he was furious and very indignant, and mocked the Jews. And he spoke before his brethren and the army of Samaria, and said, 'What are these feeble Jews doing? Will they fortify themselves? Will they offer sacrifices? Will they complete it in a day? Will they revive the stones from the heaps of rubbish—stones that are burned?' Now Tobiah the Ammonite was beside him, and he said, 'Whatever they build, if even a fox goes up on it, he will break down their stone wall.' Hear, O our God, for we are despised; turn their reproach on their own heads, and give them as plunder to a land of captivity! Do not cover their iniquity, and do not let their sin be blotted out from before

You; for they have provoked You to anger before the builders. So we built the wall, and the entire wall was joined together up to half its height, for the people had a mind to work. Now it happened, when Sanballat, Tobiah, the Arabs, the Ammonites, and the Ashdodites heard that the walls of Jerusalem were being restored and the gaps were beginning to be closed, that they became very angry, and all of them conspired together to come and attack Jerusalem and create confusion. Nevertheless we made our prayer to our God, and because of them we set a watch against them day and night."

I want us to see several key truths of spiritual warfare in this passage of Scripture. The first is, when God calls us, the opposition will oppose us. So be mindful of the opposition. Be ready for insults. The antagonists mocked and they maligned them. This is a common tactic. Be prepared for the intimidation. Be prepared for violence. They're going to threaten violence. Look at verse 11: "And our adversaries said, 'They will neither know nor see anything, till we come into their midst and kill them and cause the work to cease.'" You see fear is what causes us to cease from the work. That's why Nehemiah was preparing them for the opposition. I know this sounds like we're reading the newspaper, but it is the reality of where we live and where our nation is. This is what Jesus warned us about.

So we must be aware of the opposition, but we must also be mindful of the second key truth: the Lord's power and provision. We must first be mindful of His call, the fact that this is indeed the Lord's mission. Notice what Nehemiah said in his prayer in verse 5: "Do not cover their iniquity, and do not let their sin be blotted out from before You; for they have provoked You to anger before the builders." You see, this was God's work, and they were opposing God. Nehemiah continued in verse 9: "Nevertheless we made our prayer to our God, and because of them we set a watch against them day and night." He didn't go into panic mode. Why? God is the source of strength and power. And because of this, they had the courage to do their part. Having prayed and prepared, they did something practical. They set a watch. They put action to their faith in God, which is what we all must do.

Also, be mindful of God's provision. Jump forward with me to 6:9. It says, "For they all were trying to make us afraid, saying, 'Their hands will be weakened in the work, and it will not be done.' Now therefore, O God, strengthen my hands." Again, Ephesians 6:10 says, "Be strong in the Lord and in the power of His might."

Then we need to be mindful of our responsibility to keep praying. We noted this when we went through the first two chapters of Nehemiah. One of the characteristics of Nehemiah was he was a man of prayer. We need to be a people of prayer when the opposition comes, and it's going to come. Count on it. We need to pray because that is connecting with our source of strength. It keeps us from becoming discouraged as Jesus talked about in Luke 18. And then we need to keep building. So, it's not just prayer, but it's action. Nehemiah 4:6 begins, "So we built the wall . . . ." They prayed, and then they built the wall.

The enemy wants us to stop. We need to keep going. See the good thing is, when we're busy about our task, we have less time to dwell on the opposition. And then we just need to keep standing. Again, look back at verse 9: "Nevertheless we made our prayer to our God, and because of them we set a watch against them day and night." And now verse 13: "Therefore I positioned men behind the lower parts of the wall, at the openings; and I set the people according to their families, with their swords, their spears, and their bows." It was a family affair, and everybody was involved in the work. Now look at verse 16: "So it was, from that time on, that half of my servants worked at construction, while the other half held the spears, the shields, the bows, and wore armor; and the leaders were behind all the house of Judah. Those who built on the wall, and those who carried burdens, loaded themselves so that with one hand they worked at construction, and with the other held a weapon. Every one of the builders had his sword girded at his side as he built. And the one who sounded the trumpet was beside me." Look, we've got work to do. We have been given a mission as followers of Jesus Christ, and we've got to stay at that mission.

We are also to keep the unity. Look at verses 19–20: "Then I said to the nobles, the rulers, and the rest of the people, 'The work is great and extensive, and we are separated far from one another on the wall. Wherever you hear the sound of the trumpet, rally to us there. Our God will fight for us.'" You see, in unity we find the power and the strength of God. And as believers, we need to work toward unity by helping and encouraging one another.

I think one of the best illustrations that helps us build unity is Paul's analogy of the body. He says, in essence, there are many members and yet one body (see 1 Cor. 12:12). This translates to the body of Christ, which is the church. While we may have different functions in the body of Christ, we are one body, and we need to support the other members of the body. Even when we don't agree sometimes on the minor things, we do need to be in unity. And the key to unity? Truth, and truth is the Word of God. We can never sacrifice truth for unity; it is a byproduct of the truth.

Here's the final point, and I jump ahead again to chapter 6 where it talks about focusing. Sanballat, Tobiah, and Geshem, this unholy trinity, tried to get Nehemiah to come down off the wall and meet with them. They conspired against him. And Nehemiah said, "So I sent messengers to them, saying, 'I am doing a great work, so that I cannot come down. Why should the work cease while I leave it and go down to you?'" (v. 3). You and I have a responsibility to keep our focus. Don't chase squirrels. Be focused.

We don't have to answer to the world for everything we're doing. I've gotten to the point where I don't even return calls to the secular media because they have become the opposition party to anything morally good. So I don't even bother talking to them. I'll talk to the media that I know believers will listen to or watch. But the rest of it, why bother? It's an effort to distract us from the work that God has called us to.

So be mindful that you and I have a responsibility to keep praying, keep building, keep standing, keep the unity based upon the truth of God's Word, and keep our focus on what God has called us to do. And when God calls, and we arise and obey, expect the enemy to arise and oppose. But we must remember the greatness of our God and the importance of our cause. Finally, in all of this, we must persist.

Questions for Reflection and Discussion

1. Faced with a possible attack, what did Nehemiah lead the people to do (see v. 9)?

2. When enemies threatened, the work began to slow, and the people became discouraged, how did Nehemiah rally them (see v. 14)?
   a. Do not be afraid of them.
   b. Remember the Lord, who is great and awesome.
   c. Fight for your brothers, your sons, your daughters, your wives, and your homes.
   d. All of the above.

Notes on Today's Bible Reading

— DAY 6 —

Today's Reading: Nehemiah 5

Verse of the Day

Then I said, "What you are doing [is] not good. Should you not walk in the fear of our God because of the reproach of the nations, our enemies?"

Nehemiah 5:9

Please read the entire Scripture selection in your own Bible and highlight or underline verses that stand out to you before you read the observations and engage the questions below.

In the 1992 presidential campaign, James Carville, an advisor to Bill Clinton (who went on to win the election), coined the saying "It's the economy, stupid." He had the message posted above the door at the campaign headquarters to keep the campaign focused on the economy, something people cared about. While I don't agree with the underlying premise that the economy is the most important thing, I must admit it was a smart political move and led to their political success. The reason they succeeded is it is a rubber-meets-the-road, everyday life issue. People are impacted by the economy. But what impacts the economy? It is the moral underpinnings that are neglected, leaving the economic policies superficial at best.

The people in Nehemiah's day were reeling from a bad economy, so bad they had to sell their property and even their children
into slavery just to pay their taxes. Nehemiah didn't create a government program to alleviate the suffering, which was real; he went to
the heart of the matter—a violation of God's instruction. So I want
us to see four main points in this chapter: the rift, the reason, the
response, and finally the resolve, of Nehemiah.

First, notice the *rift*. It is evident in verse 1: "And there was
a great outcry of the people and their wives against their Jewish
brethren." There was a rift between the people over the growing
economic divide. The rich got richer, and the poor got poorer.
Something wasn't right. Nehemiah explained further in verses 2–4:
"For there were those who said, 'We, our sons, and our daughters
[are] many; therefore let us get grain, that we may eat and live.'
There were also [some] who said, 'We have mortgaged our lands
and vineyards and houses, that we might buy grain because of the
famine.' There were also those who said, 'We have borrowed money
for the king's tax [on] our lands and vineyards.'" They conclude their
complaint in verse 5: "Yet now our flesh [is] as the flesh of our
brethren, our children as their children; and indeed we are forcing
our sons and our daughters to be slaves, and [some] of our daughters have been brought into slavery. [It is] not in our power [to
redeem them], for other men have our lands and vineyards."

So how did Nehemiah respond to this charge of injustice? Look
at verse 6: "And I became very angry when I heard their outcry
and these words." This rift caused by the nobles taking advantage
of common people during a bad economy threatened to derail the
entire rebuilding and restoration project. What outsiders like Sanballat and Tobiah were unable to do to stop the building of the wall,
the internal disunity threatened to do.

That brings us to the *reason*. Nehemiah takes on the leaders in
verses 7–9.

After serious thought, I rebuked the nobles and rulers, and said to them, "Each of you is exacting usury from his brother." So I called a great assembly against them. And I said to them, "According to our ability we have redeemed our Jewish brethren who were sold to the nations. Now indeed, will you even sell your brethren? Or should they be sold to us?" Then they were silenced and found nothing [to say]. Then I said, "What you are doing [is] not good. Should you not walk in the fear of our God because of the reproach of the nations, our enemies? I also, [with] my brethren and my servants, am lending them money and grain. Please, let us stop this usury!"

This is what happens when economic gain is the sole driver. Nehemiah basically said, "Look, we've been redeemed from the bondage of a foreign nation, and now through greed we are putting our people back into bondage, to ourselves." The reason is they were not following the clear directions of God. The moral foundation of their economy had been lost.

Charging interest to their fellow citizens was prohibited in the law of God (Lev. 25:36), and they were not to be enslaving their own people. Admittedly, capitalism is an economic system fueled by a desire for gain, but it works if that desire for gain is kept in check by objective morality. If it is kept in check, it is the best economic system in existence. If not, it is subject to greed and injustice. That was happening in Nehemiah's day, all because their greed was not being restrained by obedience to God's instruction. That was the reason.

Next we see the *response*. Notice how Nehemiah deals with these leaders in verse 11: "Restore now to them, even this day, their lands, their vineyards, their olive groves, and their houses, also a hundredth of the money and the grain, the new wine and the oil, that you have charged them." Notice it wasn't enough to say, "We are sorry." Again, we see the penalty of the sin in the sin. By violating God's instruction on charging interest and on enslaving their fellow Jews, they were throwing their economy out of balance. According to a report from the International Monetary Fund, Americans' debt level is higher than it was before the Great Depression. The IMF devoted two chapters in a report on Global Financial Stability on household debt, pointing out that high debt level tends to make economic downturns deeper and more prolonged.[1] God's way clearly is best.

In response to Nehemiah's directive, we see in verse 12: "So they said, 'We will restore [it], and will require nothing from them; we will do as you say.'" Nehemiah wasted no time to allow them to backtrack in verse 12b: "Then I called the priests, and required an oath from them that they would do according to this promise." But Nehemiah went even further in verse 13: "Then I shook out the fold of my garment and said, 'So may God shake out each man from his house, and from his property, who does not perform this promise. Even thus may he be shaken out and emptied.' And all the assembly said, 'Amen!' and praised the Lord. Then the people did according to this promise." It is clear that Nehemiah wanted them to keep their promise.

Finally, I want us to see the *resolve* of Nehemiah. Look at verses 14–16.

> Moreover, from the time that I was appointed to be their governor in the land of Judah, from the twentieth year until the thirty-second year of King Artaxerxes, twelve years, neither I nor my brothers ate the governor's provisions. But the former governors who [were] before me laid burdens on the people, and took from them bread and wine, besides

forty shekels of silver. Yes, even their servants bore rule over the people, but I did not do so, because of the fear of God. Indeed, I also continued the work on this wall, and we did not buy any land. All my servants [were] gathered there for the work.

Don't miss this: "because of the fear of God." The Hebrew word *yiraw* means an intense reverence and respect for God. Because of that, look at what Nehemiah and his team did in verses 17–18: "And at my table [were] one hundred and fifty Jews and rulers, besides those who came to us from the nations around us. Now [that] which was prepared daily [was] one ox [and] six choice sheep. Also fowl were prepared for me, and once every ten days an abundance of all kinds of wine. Yet in spite of this I did not demand the governor's provisions, because the bondage was heavy on this people."

Not only did Nehemiah not take, but he gave. He did not want to add to the burden of the people. He simply wanted to serve them. He didn't take advantage of the economic opportunities they had at the expense of the hurting people. Nehemiah and his team had an eternal perspective. How do I know this? Jump down to the very last verse where Nehemiah prays, "Remember me, my God, for good, [according to] all that I have done for this people" (v. 19).

This is something I need to be reminded of daily. As much as we like to see a return on our investment today and see our efforts acknowledged and rewarded, it doesn't always occur. Nehemiah continued to face opposition, libelous accusations, and even threats. He knew that even if they put a plaque on the wall that said, "Governor Nehemiah built this wall in 444 BC," it wouldn't be long until his sacrifices were forgotten. God, however, does not forget. Though He will forget our sins covered by the blood of Jesus Christ, He will not forget our service done in the name of Jesus Christ.

Questions for Reflection and Discussion

1. What was the outcry against the nobles and rulers during difficult economic times?

2. What example did Nehemiah set when he became governor (see 5:14–19)?
   a. Refused to take pay traditionally given to governors
   b. Declined to buy up cheap land and evict the poor
   c. Stayed on mission and kept working on the wall
   d. Showed personal generosity during hard times
   e. All of the above

Notes on Today's Bible Reading

_____

_____

_____

_____

_____

_____

_____

_____

_____

_____

_____

_____

_____

_____

— DAY 7 —
Today's Reading: Nehemiah 6

Verse of the Day

> So I sent messengers to them, saying, "I am doing a great work, so that I cannot come down. Why should the work cease while I leave it and go down to you?"
>
> *Nehemiah 6:3*

Please read the entire Scripture selection in your own Bible and highlight or underline verses that stand out to you before you read the observations and engage the questions below.

Charles Spurgeon once said, "Discernment is not knowing the difference between right and wrong. It is knowing the difference between right and almost right." You know, the black and white issues are easy to discern right from wrong. But increasingly in a world that's turned gray, sometimes it's hard to tell the difference in the right thing to do and the almost right thing. With that said, in our world it is imperative that we learn to use discernment.

Look at Nehemiah 6:1–2: "Now it happened when Sanballat, Tobiah, Geshem the Arab, and the rest of our enemies heard that I had rebuilt the wall, and that there were no breaks left in it(though at that time I had not hung the doors in the gates), that Sanballat and Geshem sent to me, saying, 'Come, let us meet together among the villages in the plain of Ono.' But they thought to do me harm."

Now, think about this. This wall was being built, and yet Nehemiah had all this opposition. They were scaring people. We would describe their acts today as acts of terrorism. And so, they sent to him what appeared to be an olive branch. "Let's meet in the plain of Ono," they said. If anyone ever invites you to Ono, just say no.

Was it a bad thing for him to make peace with his enemies? I mean, aren't we supposed to make peace with our enemies? This is where discernment comes in because making peace with our enemies is a good thing. But was it the *best* thing to do in Nehemiah's case? Is it what God told Nehemiah to do? He had to discern that what they wanted to do was harm him.

Oftentimes for a leader, the choice is not between what is good and bad but, rather, what is good and best. And this is why a leader needs discernment. We need to ask, "Is this what God wants?" We must discern what is best as opposed to what might be good; a short-term outcome of peace can often lead to complete and total conflict and unrest. Nehemiah said in verse 12, "Then I perceived, I discerned that God had not sent him at all, but that he pronounced this prophecy against me because Tobiah and Sanballat had hired him." He's referring to this would-be prophet who came and looked quite holy (vv. 6–13). He put the "thee and the thou" in there, so it sounded like it was really from God. "Thou shouldest" must be from God, right? That's old King James. The reality is, we must try to continually practice discernment because at times deception comes packaged not with a neon light saying, "I'm here to deceive you and mislead you"; it comes in quite a convincing, compelling package. For Nehemiah, one came as if he were a prophet from the Lord, speaking as if he were sent from the Lord.

It sounds like from this passage that Nehemiah had to hesitate for just a moment. Notice he says, "But then I perceived." This suggests to me there was a moment when Nehemiah wondered, *Well, I don't know. Maybe, just maybe, this guy is for real. But then again, maybe not. I need to know if this is of God.* Based on what we know of Nehemiah, what do you think he did? He prayed. Absolutely, I can guarantee you, he prayed. He says, "but then I perceived that God had not sent him at all, but that he pronounces prophecy against me because Tobiah and Sanballat had hired him. For this reason He was hired that I should be afraid and act in that way and sin, so that they might have calls for an evil report that they might reproach me." See, a leader understands that sometimes things are not as they may seem.

The only way we have that level of discernment is from the Holy Spirit. And the only way we have the presence of the Holy Spirit in our life is we must spend time in the presence of God in His Word. We cannot be compromised in our life, meaning we are willfully disobeying God. If you are intentionally disobeying God, you will not have the discernment of the Holy Spirit. And by that I do not mean the occasional slip up or a sin you are fighting against but have not yet conquered; I am talking about willful, deliberate sin. If this is where you are in your life, why would God help you discern? If He has clearly made something available to you and you've rejected it, essentially, you have said, "God, I don't care what you say." So if we want the discernment of the Holy Spirit, we must walk in obedience to God.

There are natural abilities to discern, and there is the spiritual gift of discernment. Some people have greater levels of discernment, but all of us as believers can have discernment and should have discernment—and we should pray and seek discernment. In my experience, women are especially gifted with discernment. For some reason, I find that wives are more discerning than their husbands. Men, that's a nod you should listen to your wives on these issues. They generally have a sense about them of greater discernment. Consequently, we as leaders, we must pray for and learn to develop discernment.

How do we gain the type of discernment that Nehemiah had? Now, remember, I go back to what I said at the very beginning: Nehemiah did not set out to go to Jerusalem to be a leader; he set out on a mission to build a wall. This was a burden God had given him. And so, people began to gather around him because of the goal.

Here's how we develop discernment: Proverbs 28:7 says, "Whosoever keeps the law is a discerning son, but a companion of glutton shames his father." This is what we were talking about. We must obey the Word of God. Psalm 119:66 says, "Teach me good judgment and knowledge, for I believe your commandments." If we don't start by obeying what God has presented to us with great clarity and in abundance in the Word of God, He's not going to give us anything in addition to that. Now, the Holy Spirit will lead us into all understanding of the truth, but we must live out the truth we already know before He will reveal even more (see John 14:21). Discernment begins by knowing and obeying the Word of God. And a leader must have discernment. Pray for it and live in alignment with God's Word, and He will graciously grant it.

Questions for Reflection and Discussion

1. How did Nehemiah respond to the invitation of his enemies?

2. When the plot to take his life began coming to light, what did Nehemiah do?
   a. Arm himself with more weapons
   b. Assign more guards
   c. Ask God for His help
   d. None of the above

Notes on Today's Bible Reading

_____

_____

_____

_____

_____

_____

_____

_____

_____

_____

_____

_____

_____

_____

_____

_____

_____

_____

— DAY 8 —
Today's Reading: Nehemiah 7

Verse of the Day

I gave my brother Hanani and Hananiah the governor of the castle charge over Jerusalem, for he was a more faithful and God-fearing man than many.

Nehemiah 7:2

Please read the entire Scripture selection in your own Bible and highlight or underline verses that stand out to you before you read the observations and engage the questions below.

Today we are in Nehemiah 7. This is the roll call of the families who came back from the captivity in Babylon. An almost identical list is found in Ezra 2. When we come across a list of names like this, most of us are inclined to skip it and move on. But we should always ask the question, why is it here? If it was not important, would God have preserved it for us? A general observation is, this list reminds us that God knows our name. Every individual and family matters. In verse 64, those who were not on the list were excluded from the priesthood: "These sought their registration among those enrolled in the genealogies, but it was not found there, so they were excluded from the priesthood as unclean." That seems a bit harsh. Maybe it was an administrative oversight. Or maybe someone just skipped the registration line on their way out of Babylon. It is a reminder there are no cutting corners with God. Yes, He is merciful, but He is just.

Peter described followers of Jesus in 1 Peter 2:9 this way: "But you are a chosen generation, a royal priesthood, a holy nation, His own special people, that you may proclaim the praises of Him who called you out of darkness into His marvelous light." This is true not of those who are simply in the congregation or show up at church; it is for those who have made Jesus Christ their Savior and Lord, whose names are written in the Lamb's book of life.

Look with me at Nehemiah 7:1–2: "Now when the wall had been built and I had set up the doors, and the gatekeepers, the singers, and the Levites had been appointed, I gave my brother Hanani and Hananiah the governor of the castle charge over Jerusalem, for he was a more faithful and God-fearing man than many." It is thought by a number of scholars that Nehemiah was setting things in order to prepare for a return to Shushan as he had promised the king. So he was putting qualified leadership in place to attend to the well-being of Jerusalem.

Notice that Nehemiah appointed two men as governors or consuls. The first was his brother Hanani, who initially brought news to him of the situation in Jerusalem. It is a joy when family members can work together in unity, especially for the kingdom of God. I've had that opportunity a couple of times, to work with family, and there is a level of trust rarely found in other relationships. Yet Nehemiah found it in Hananiah, who had been ruler of the palace. Two qualifying descriptors of Hananiah are (1) he was faithful, and (2) He was God-fearing. Being faithful in the small things prepares us and qualifies us for the more significant tasks. Remember what Jesus said in the parable of the talents: "His lord said to him, 'Well done, good and faithful servant; you were faithful over a few things, I will make you ruler over many things. Enter into the joy of your lord'" (Matt. 25:21). When we do our work as unto the Lord, He does not overlook those who are faithful (see Col. 3:23–24). There were many who feared the Lord, which was good and essential for the restoration of Jerusalem, but it was said that Hananiah feared God "more than many." What does this mean? What does this look like?

I assume Hananiah was a devout man whose allegiance to God was evident in his public conduct, and it also ran deep. His holiness and devotion to God didn't stop when he was no longer in the public's eye, but his devotion to God is what caused him to walk upright before others. Nehemiah, knowing full well the challenges of leading, needed men who could withstand the temptations and the testing that would come. These are qualities we should look for when we select leaders, whether they be in the church, society, or business.

In 7:3, Nehemiah gives them this charge: "'Do not let the gates of Jerusalem be opened until the sun is hot; and while they stand guard, let them shut and bar the doors; and appoint guards from among the inhabitants of Jerusalem, one at his watch station and another in front of his own house.'" The walls had been built, but the threat was not gone. When we accept Jesus as our Savior and submit to Him as the Lord of our lives, we see the ruins of our life restored, but we must remain vigilant and aware of the spiritual threats that exist and desire to invade, destroy, and rob us of the joy and peace God has provided.

Questions for Reflection and Discussion

1. What qualities did Nehemiah note in Hananiah that would make him a good leader (7:2)?

2. With the walls completed in an astounding fifty-two days, what did God prompt Nehemiah to do next (7:5)?
   - a. Take a week off
   - b. Go on a trip
   - c. Register the people by genealogy
   - d. None of the above

Notes on Today's Bible Reading

— DAY 9 —

Today's Reading: Nehemiah 8

Verse of the Day

> Then he said to them, "Go your way, eat the fat, drink the sweet, and send portions to those for whom nothing is prepared; for this day is holy to our Lord. Do not sorrow, for the joy of the LORD is your strength."
>
> *Nehemiah 8:10*

Please read the entire Scripture selection in your own Bible and highlight or underline verses that stand out to you before you read the observations and engage the questions below.

Nehemiah was an example, I think, of a truly great leader, as was Ezra, the priest. He had returned to Jerusalem thirteen years before Nehemiah. But Nehemiah did something Ezra had not yet done. I understand that Nehemiah was there to take charge and rebuild the wall. But in this chapter, the work on the wall was done. So he turned his focus to the greatest threat the people faced: spiritual compromise and complacency. And he turned to the Word of God. You see, a truly great leader understands the importance of the spiritual well-being of the people.

We aren't told everything in the book of Nehemiah, but through this two-month experience of rallying the people to tackle this monumental problem, repelling the nonstop harassment and attacks of the opposition, then having to tend to the fissures within his own ranks, Nehemiah realized these people had some deeper problems that needed to be dealt with at this point. First, their need for temporal security had to be met. Now that they were secure behind walls, they could focus on the spiritual needs without fear. So Nehemiah turned to the only place where individuals, families, communities, and nations can truly be rebuilt: the Word of God. That's where he directed their attention.

We need to start with the last verse of the previous chapter to really set the stage for this. Take a look at the second half of Nehemiah 7:73: "When the seventh month came, the children of Israel were in their cities." The seventh month was the Feast of the Trumpets or, literally, the day of shouting and blasting. The first day of the seventh month signaled the beginning of the new year. The seventh month began with the Feast of Trumpets, followed by the Day of Atonement, followed by the Feast of Tabernacles. And this was something the people had not observed for quite some time, as we'll read here in a moment.

Next, let's look at Nehemiah 8:1, "Now all the people gathered together as one man in the open square that was in front of the Water Gate; and they told Ezra the scribe to bring the Book of the Law of Moses, which the LORD had commanded Israel." Notice it says they had gathered as "one man," which means they were unified. They had a single focus in what they were doing. The challenges of rebuilding the wall required a unified effort.

And remember the opposition? The people had a trowel in one hand and a sword in the other. They were having to fend off the opposition that wanted to stop them, and their opponents did not want them to enjoy security. It's a great picture, by the way, of the spiritual battle we're in today. They were in a physical battle, but as we try to build the walls around our family, we're faced with spiritual opposition, and we must have a sword. What is the sword? It's the Word of God.

Let's move on to verses 2–4a: "So Ezra the priest brought the Law before the assembly of men and women and all who could hear with understanding on the first day of the seventh month. Then he read from it in the open square that was in front of the Water Gate from morning until midday, before the men and women and those who could understand; and the ears of all the people were attentive to the Book of the Law. So Ezra the scribe stood on a platform of wood which they had made for the purpose." This is the first we see of a pulpit for the presentation of the Word of God in Scripture.

Then in verses 5–8:

> And Ezra opened the book in the sight of all the people, for he was standing above all the people; and when he opened it, all the people stood up. And Ezra blessed the LORD, the great God. Then all the people answered, 'Amen, Amen!' while lifting up their hands. And they bowed their heads and worshiped the LORD with their faces to the ground.
>
> Also Jeshua, Bani, Sherebiah, Jamin, Akkub, Shabbethai, Hodijah, Maaseiah, Kelita, Azariah, Jozabad, Hanan, Pelaiah, and the Levites, helped the people to understand the Law; and the people stood in their place. So they read distinctly from the book, in the Law of God; and they gave the sense, and helped them to understand the reading.

The Levites were small-group leaders who helped the people understand what they had just heard. A vibrant church is going to have a focus on biblical understanding because that's the key to spiritual growth and development. You cannot have a strong, vibrant church, community, or family without the Word of God. It's central to this.

Today, churches may call it Sunday school, small groups, or Bible study groups. It doesn't matter what you call it, but it should be a study on the Word of God. Some of these small groups spend a lot more time in "prayer requests" than they do studying the Word of God. And that's one of the reasons we are doing this journey through the Bible. It's essential that believers be in the Word, studying it. And it's thrilling to see people's lives transformed and empowered by God's Word.

Let's continue in Nehemiah 8:9–11:

> And Nehemiah, who was the governor, Ezra the priest and scribe, and the Levites who taught the people said to all the people, "This day is holy to the LORD your God; do not mourn nor weep." For all the people wept, when they heard the words of the Law. Then he said to them, "Go your way, eat the fat, drink the sweet, and send portions to those for whom nothing is prepared; for this day is holy to our Lord. Do not sorrow, for the joy of the LORD is your strength." So the Levites quieted all the people, saying, "Be still, for the day is holy; do not be grieved."

You see, some of them were hearing the Word for the very first time. They didn't have Bibles they could pull off the shelf, they didn't have smart phones with a Bible app, they didn't have a radio or television they could turn on. They didn't have the Internet where they could search and do a journey through the Bible. They were hearing it the only way they could.

That's why these festivals were so important. They gathered, and the Word of God was read to them. As I said, for some of them, it was the first time they heard it. They then realized how far they had strayed from God, and they wept. The soil of their heart was being tilled. They were being prepared for repentance, which we'll see soon. This, frankly, is the power of the Word of God. This is what Paul wrote about in Romans. Look at Romans 10:14: "How then shall they call on Him in whom they have not believed? And how shall they believe in Him of whom they have not heard? And how shall they hear without a preacher?" The Word is critical.

The Feast of Trumpets was a joyous occasion. That's why they said, "Don't, don't grieve, don't weep. The joy of the Lord is your strength." The Day of Atonement, which was coming, was the day to weep and fast, but the feast was a day of rejoicing. Look at verses 12–16:

> And all the people went their way to eat and drink, to send portions and rejoice greatly, because they understood the words that were declared to them. Now on the second day the heads of the fathers' houses of all the people, with the priests and Levites, were gathered to Ezra the scribe, in order to understand the words of the Law. And they found written in the Law, which the LORD had commanded by Moses, that the children of Israel should dwell in booths during the feast of the seventh month, and that they should announce and proclaim in all their cities and in Jerusalem, saying, "Go out to the mountain, and bring olive branches, branches of oil trees, myrtle branches, palm branches, and branches of leafy trees, to make booths, as it is written." Then the people went out and brought them and made themselves booths, each one on the roof of his house, or in their courtyards or the courts of the house of God, and in the open square of the Water Gate and in the open square of the Gate of Ephraim.

Nehemiah and Ezra had to have been thrilled. This is what every teacher or preacher of the Word of God wants to see people acting on: the Word of God. They didn't say, "Oh, well, we read this and this is already upon us. We really don't have time to do it. Let's make preparations for next year." No, they went and they did it. Look at verse 17: "So the whole assembly of those who had returned from the captivity made booths and sat under the booths; for since the days of Joshua the son of Nun until that day the children of Israel had not done so. And there was very great gladness."

It says there was great gladness. Obedience brings gladness. There are innumerable intangible benefits that come from obeying God and not the least of which is joy. Look at verse 18: "Also day by day, from the first day until the last day, he read from the Book of the Law of God. And they kept the feast seven days; and on the eighth day there was a sacred assembly, according to the prescribed manner."

What a great chapter! What a great example of leadership, a civil leader, the governor coming there to rebuild the wall, a great construction project. Nehemiah, however, didn't neglect the true needs of the people, and that was the spiritual foundation. That's where our true protection lies: in standing on the Word of God.

Questions for Reflection and Discussion

1. Once the walls were completed, what did Ezra and the Levites do at the people's request (see vv. 1–8)?
   a. Opened the Word of God and read for six hours
   b. Taught all who could understand
   c. Led the people to bless the God of heaven
   d. Helped the people understand with a view toward application
   e. All of the above

2. When the people wept because of their sins exposed by the Word, what did the leaders command that they do first (see v.10), and what festival did they celebrate (see vv. 13–18)?

Notes on Today's Bible Reading

— DAY 10 —

Today's Reading: Nehemiah 9

Verse of the Day

And they stood up in their place and read from the Book of the Law of the Lord their God for one-fourth of the day; and for another fourth they confessed and worshiped the Lord their God.

Nehemiah 9:3

Please read the entire Scripture selection in your own Bible and highlight or underline verses that stand out to you before you read the observations and engage the questions below.

Today we study Nehemiah 9, and if I gave the study a title it would be "Stand and Confess." As the people heard the Word of God, their hearts were stirred, and they responded with weeping, as we read in chapter 8. However, they were observing the Feast of Tabernacles, which was a time to celebrate the deliverance and provision of the Lord, so they were told not to weep but to allow the joy of the Lord to be their strength. Now, two days after the Feast of Tabernacles, we have a solemn time of fasting that led to a confession of their sin against God, a confession of their history with God, and a confession of returning to God.

First, notice how they came before the Lord, confessing their sins against God, going back to their forefathers in verses 1–3:

"Now on the twenty-fourth day of this month the children of Israel were assembled with fasting, in sackcloth, and with dust on their heads. Then those of Israelite lineage separated themselves from all foreigners; and they stood and confessed their sins and the iniquities of their fathers. And they stood up in their place and read from the Book of the Law of the LORD their God for one-fourth of the day; and for another fourth they confessed and worshiped the LORD their God."

In Romans 2, Paul wrote about the goodness or kindness of God leading us to repentance. This is what we see in Nehemiah 9, as the people just finished one of the three pilgrimage festivals that came after the time of harvest, a time of celebrating God's blessings. The eight priests listed may have alternated, or the congregation may have been broken into smaller prayer groups; but what we see next is their praise in verses 5b–6: "Blessed be Your glorious name, which is exalted above all blessing and praise! You alone are the LORD; You have made heaven, the heaven of heavens, with all their host, the earth and everything on it, the seas and all that is in them, and You preserve them all. The host of heaven worships You." There are four things they were saying about God: (1) God is Lord alone; (2) God is the Creator of all things; (3) God is the sustainer of all things; and (4) God is the one to be worshipped.

Second, notice how the leader of this prayer began confessing their history with God as a people. Verses 7–35 are a history lesson from the beginning to the present state of their nation in Nehemiah's day—the good, the bad, and the ugly. Let's begin with verses 7–10:

"You are the LORD God, who chose Abram, and brought him out of Ur of the Chaldeans, and gave him the name Abraham; You found his heart faithful before You, and made a covenant with him to give the land of the Canaanites, the Hittites, the Amorites, the Perizzites, the Jebusites, and the Girgashites—to give it to his descendants. You have performed Your words, for You are righteous. You saw the affliction of our fathers in Egypt, and heard their cry by the Red Sea. You showed signs and wonders against Pharaoh, against all his servants, and against all the people of his land. For You knew that they acted proudly against them. So You made a name for Yourself, as it is this day."

Remember, this was a priest—some suggest Ezra—praying to God, recounting His faithfulness and the people's repeated faithlessness. Throughout the Bible, we find a periodic recounting of Israel's history, such as Psalm 105 or Stephen's sermon in Acts 7. In Nehemiah 9, this was probably top of mind at this moment as the Feast of the Tabernacles had just concluded. This was a large portion of the reason for the feast, to remind them of their history, who they were, and what God had done for them.

Our history shapes who we are, which directs our future. This is why there is such an effort to rewrite our history and create a new narrative. Have you heard of the 1619 Project? It removes Christianity, God, and the Bible from our history so that we are left with no identity or a deceptively altered identity. That's why we need to recover our true history as Americans—all of it.

In the prayer, Nehemiah's people looked back to the Patriarchs: Abraham, Isaac, and Jacob. We look back to Founding Fathers like George Washington, Samuel Adams, Patrick Henry as well as other leaders such as Lincoln, Roosevelt, and Reagan—all flawed but God-fearing men. Our founding document, the Declaration of Independence, is really a "Declaration of Dependence" on God. It references God four times, concluding "with a firm reliance on the protection of divine Providence, we mutually pledge to each other our Lives, our Fortunes and our sacred Honor."[2] Founding Father John Adams said this about our governing document, the U.S.

Constitution: "Our Constitution was made only for a moral and religious people. It is wholly inadequate to the government of any other."[3] We remove this identity, with its biblical foundations and all the virtues and values from our history and culture, at our peril.

Third, the leader next confessed their return to God. Look down at how they formalize it at the end of the chapter (vv. 36–38): "'Here we are, servants today! And the land that You gave to our fathers, to eat its fruit and its bounty, here we are, servants in it! And it yields much increase to the kings You have set over us, because of our sins; also they have dominion over our bodies and our cattle at their pleasure; and we are in great distress. And because of all this, we make a sure covenant and write it; our leaders, our Levites, and our priests seal it.'"

Notice there was no shifting of the blame or rationalizing their situation. They connected their present situation with their persistent sin. This was not one of those, "If we've offended you God, we are sorry." It was, "We have sinned against you, and we ask for your mercy." Knowing their history with God enabled them to confess their desire to return to Him boldly. I pray our history with God as Americans will motivate more of us to do the same.

Questions for Reflection and Discussion

1. After the celebration, there was a solemn assembly that included what activities?
   a. Assembled with fasting and in sackcloth
   b. Separated themselves from all foreigners
   c. Confessed their sins and the iniquities of their fathers
   d. Worshipped the Lord their God
   e. All of the above

2. After the prayer of repentance in verses 5–37, what did the leaders resolve to do (v. 38)?

Notes on Today's Bible Reading

— DAY 11 —

Today's Reading: Nehemiah 10

Verse of the Day

[T]hese joined with their brethren, their nobles, and entered into a curse and an oath to walk in God's Law, which was given by Moses the servant of God, and to observe and do all the commandments of the LORD our Lord, and His ordinances and His statutes.

Nehemiah 10:29

Please read the entire Scripture selection in your own Bible and highlight or underline verses that stand out to you before you read the observations and engage the questions below.

When is the old better than the new? Let's find out. Today we are in Nehemiah 10, but first recall in chapter 8, those who had returned to Jerusalem from captivity rediscovered the Word of God as Ezra read it to them. For some, this may have been the very first time they read or heard the law of God read to them. In chapter 9, repentance of their sin was the evidence that they were truly listening to the reading of God's Word. And now here in chapter 10, we see further evidence of the fact they were listening to the Word of God because they acted upon their repentance by renewing their covenant with God.

The process here is important. In Matthew 12:43–45 Jesus said, "When an unclean spirit goes out of a man, he goes through dry places, seeking rest, and finds none. Then he says, 'I will return to my house from which I came.' And when he comes, he finds it empty, swept, and put in order. Then he goes and takes with him seven other spirits more wicked than himself, and they enter and dwell there; and the last state of that man is worse than the first. So shall it also be with this wicked generation." In other words, when evil is removed, repented of, it must be replaced with that which is good; or the evil will return, and it will be worse than it was before.

When we respond to God's Word with repentance, that's good. Absolutely good. But there's more. We must act in the affirmative to change our ways. And we see this here in Nehemiah 10. The people didn't stop with repentance only. They replaced their evil or sinful practices with that which was good. Look at verse 1: "Now those who placed their seal on the document were: Nehemiah the governor, the son of Hacaliah, and Zedekiah, . . ." Here it talks about the seal. They had basically put their signature to this declaration that they were going to follow God.

The first twenty-eight verses list all the names of the elders—not all of the people but the leaders of the people—so let's drop down to Nehemiah 10:29–32:

These joined with their brethren, their nobles, and entered into a curse and an oath to walk in God's Law, which was given by Moses the servant of God, and to observe and do all the commandments of the Lord our Lord, and His ordinances and His statutes: We would not give our daughters as wives to the peoples of the land, nor take their daughters for our sons; if the peoples of the land brought wares or any grain to sell on the Sabbath day, we would not buy it from them on the Sabbath, or on a holy day; and we would forego the seventh year's produce and the exacting of every debt. Also we made ordinances for ourselves, to exact from ourselves yearly one-third of a shekel for the service of the house of our God.

Responding to the Word of God, they repented of their sins and the sins of their fathers. But the next step we read here is not to create something new, as if the old way of their fathers, who walked with God, was outdated. They committed to walk in God's law, not some new interpretation of God's law. But as Moses had given it to them, they returned to the old way. Jeremiah 18:15 says, "'Because My people have forgotten Me, they have burned incense to worthless idols. And they have caused themselves to stumble in their ways, from the ancient paths, to walk in pathways and not on a highway." The point is, there is no new way to God. And in the Old Testament, it was returning to the law of God and walking in that.

Now I understand we're not living in Old Testament times or under the Old Testament law of Moses. We're living under the New Testament economy of grace. But here is the way in John 14:6, where Jesus said, "I am the way, the truth, and the life. No one comes to the Father except through Me." He is the only way to God. Of course, some want to redefine that and try to discover a new way or lay out a new interpretation. God's Word, however, when truly heard, leads to repentance, and that should lead to a return to the truth.

So three aspects to this renewal in Nehemiah 10 have spiritual application for us today. Number one is sanctification. What does that mean? Simply, it means being set apart, and that was a portion of this. They were going to refuse to continue their practice of intermarrying, marrying those in the pagan nations, of being unequally yoked. This practice led to the idolatry that led them into seventy years of captivity. Before you go saying, "Well, this doesn't have any application to us today," look what Paul wrote to the Corinthians over in 2 Corinthians 6:14–18:

> Do not be unequally yoked together with unbelievers. For what fellowship has righteousness with lawlessness? And what communion has light with darkness? And what accord has Christ with Belial? Or what part has a believer with an unbeliever? And what agreement has the temple of God with idols? For you are the temple of the living God. As God has said: "I will dwell in them and walk among them. I will be their God, and they shall be My people." Therefore "Come out from among them and be separate, says the Lord. Do not touch what is unclean, And I will receive you. I will be a Father to you, and you shall be My sons and daughters, says the Lord Almighty."

This is not talking only about marriage, which is obviously the most prominent example, but it speaks also of relationships that alter our walk before God. We're not to be unequally yoked, meaning walking in step with those who are not walking under the direction of the Holy Spirit because that can lead us astray. This is exactly what happened to the children of Israel, and that has application to us today.

Now let's look at the second aspect of renewal. First, we have sanctification, then we have Sabbath. Again, we're not under the law, but the observation of the Sabbath was an outward sign of trusting God. This also included the sabbatical year, when the land was allowed to rest. That meant the people wouldn't reap. They wouldn't be working the land. They would trust God to provide what they needed. Instead of working seven days a week to get ahead, they declared they would trust God to provide for them.

It is a little hard for us to truly comprehend the fullness of this commitment because we live in a time of such plenty. In those days there were no Walmarts with stocked shelves just down the street. There were no government programs. It was what they were able to raise and grow that determined what they ate. While not being legalistic, I do believe how we approach a day dedicated to the Lord, when we rest from our normal activities, remains important. And I believe the Lord gives us discretion on how we do this. But I think if we're working seven days a week and no day is set aside— dedicated to worshipping the Lord, hearing the Word taught, teaching the Word, and resting from our normal activities—it may be leading us down quite a similar path that we see with the children of Israel repeatedly.

The third aspect of renewal from this passage is service. We see the Israelites committing themselves to service. They committed to serving the Lord with their time and their resources. They were to give a shekel, but because they were impoverished, they all agreed to give a third of a shekel to the service for the house of God. And then they talked about bringing in the wood. That was going to take time and labor. And so, they committed their time and resources to the work of God, knowing it was important.

This is important for us today that, number one, we need to have a place of fellowship. I know after the pandemic many people transitioned to watching online preachers and teachers, and that's one of the positive things about what occurred in 2020. People discovered there are actually solid teachings online, and many speakers are teaching the Word of God.

We, however, need fellowship with one another, we need community, and we need to support that local community with our time and resources. As Jesus said in Matthew 6:21, "For where your treasure is, there your heart will be also." We need to be investing in the work of God in our local churches. And I encourage you to support and be a part of those churches that are preaching the Word of God, living out the Word of God, and impacting the community in the world around them. The bottom line is this: when it comes to following God, the old way of obedience to God and to His Word is not only the best way; it is the only way in which we can truly follow God and experience all He has for us.

Questions for Reflection and Discussion

1. What were the primary contents of the covenant the people made with the Lord (vv. 28–31)?
   a. To walk in God's law and do all the commandments of the Lord
   b. To forbid our children from intermarrying with the pagan neighbors
   c. To refuse to buy or sell on the Sabbath or on a holy day
   d. To forego the crops and the exaction of every debt during the Sabbath year
   e. All of the above

2. What did they promise not to neglect (v. 39)?

Notes on Today's Bible Reading

_____

_____

_____

_____

_____

_____

Nehemiah: Rebuilding a Nation

— DAY 12 —

Today's Reading: Nehemiah 11

Verse of the Day

And the people blessed all the men who willingly offered themselves to dwell at Jerusalem.

Nehemiah 11:2

Please read the entire Scripture selection in your own Bible and highlight or underline verses that stand out to you before you read the observations and engage the questions below.

Today we are in Nehemiah 11, and the message is "Arise and Occupy." This was an amazing time in the history of Israel. The return had been underway for nearly one hundred years, but it was moving in fits and starts. The first wave of Jewish exiles returning to Jerusalem was in 537 BC.[4] Construction on the temple began the next year but wasn't finished until 516 BC. Ezra brought the second wave of exiles back in 455 BC, then Nehemiah led the third wave in 445 BC. This entire time the city walls remained piles of rubble, and the city was exposed and unprotected.

Nehemiah, as we've read, led the effort to rebuild the city not only physically but spiritually, morally, and culturally. But once the city was restored and the people revived, beyond the religious and civic leaders, few were willing to occupy the city. Why did some come, and others did not?

Before we read the chapter and answer the question, let me say the answer has relevance to us today. Many are not wanting to dwell in the spiritual city of God today for the same reasons they were hesitant or unwilling in Nehemiah's day. Look at verse 1: "Now the leaders of the people dwelt at Jerusalem; the rest of the people cast lots to bring one out of ten to dwell in Jerusalem, the holy city, and nine-tenths were to dwell in other cities." What do we read here that we've not seen before in Nehemiah? Holy city. Jerusalem had now been sanctified and set apart for the Lord. In fact, this description of Jerusalem as "the holy city" only appears before this in Isaiah, describing Jerusalem after the captivity. Also, note the 10 percent, a tithe of the people, a remnant. Rarely does God use the majority.

And according to verses 2–6, some willingly offered to live in the Holy City:

> And the people blessed all the men who willingly offered themselves to dwell at Jerusalem. These *are* the heads of the province who dwelt in Jerusalem. (But in the cities of Judah everyone dwelt in his own possession in their cities—Israelites, priests, Levites, Nethinim, and descendants of Solomon's servants.) Also in Jerusalem dwelt *some* of the children of Judah and of the children of Benjamin. The children of Judah: Athaiah the son of Uzziah, the son of Zechariah, the son of Amariah, the son of Shephatiah, the son of Mahalalel, of the children of Perez; and Maaseiah the son of Baruch, the son of Col-Hozeh, the son of Hazaiah, the son of Adaiah, the son of Joiarib, the son of Zechariah, the son of Shiloni. All the sons of Perez who dwelt at Jerusalem *were* four hundred and sixty-eight valiant men.

OK, we will stop there, but we have the clues in these first eight verses that allow us to draw a reasonable conclusion as to why the people were reluctant to occupy the Holy City: fear.

You might ask, how do we know it was fear? Look at those who did occupy the city and how they are described. The sons of Perez, 468 valiant men. Strong, brave, a force, an army. (A note: Perez was the son of Judah that he had through Tamar, his daughter-in-law, which is recorded in Genesis 38. Jesus' genealogy in Matthew 1 goes back to Judah through Perez. Just another reminder of God's amazing redemption.) They were not the only ones; even the priests were described as mighty men of valor in Nehemiah 11:14. Courage led some into the city; fear kept others out.

First, there was the *fear of surrender*. The city was now a holy, sanctified city, and they were accustomed to living as they pleased. Recall the reforms that Nehemiah led them through in chapters 8 and 9; there was greater scrutiny of the way people conducted themselves in the shadow of the temple. Many today don't want to surrender their will to the will of the Father, so they stay outside the city of God.

Second, there was the *fear of man*. Up until this moment, they had seen the city lying in ruins their entire lives, a reminder of the devastation and destruction that happened 140 years before. Remember Nehemiah's description of the city, the gates burned with fire. As they went to the temple, they passed the charred remains of the gates and were reminded of the hostility of those around them and to live in the holy city marked them. Living in Jerusalem clearly identified them as Jewish.

Third, there was the *fear of the future*. The evidence and the stories of the siege that brought down Jerusalem were vivid. Living outside in the villages, you could get away or have greater economic opportunities. You wouldn't be vulnerable to an uncertain future if history were to repeat itself, which it did. So fear kept many out, and the city was only repopulated by lots. Many were invited, but few were chosen. The invitation when out to all, but fear kept most out, and so lots were cast to choose the remnant that would occupy the city.

I do want to quickly return to those who freely came into the city and were celebrated: "And the people blessed all the men who willingly offered themselves to dwell at Jerusalem" (v. 2). These were willing to live courageously, even the priests, ready to do battle. By the way, we must be willing to do spiritual battle today if we are going to occupy the city of God. They sanctified themselves, submitting to God under the scrutiny of others. They were willing to sacrifice their desires and the benefits offered by living in the cities and villages for the greater purpose of God, serving Him and others. The call to us is the same today.

Questions for Reflection and Discussion

1. For what reason did the people cast lots (see vv. 1–2)?
    a. To see who would win the big prize
    b. To decide who would move into Jerusalem
    c. To decide who would be the new mayor of Jerusalem
    d. None of the above

2. Who had oversight of the outward business of the house of God (see v. 16)?

Notes on Today's Bible Reading

_____

_____

_____

_____

— DAY 13 —
Today's Reading: Nehemiah 12

Verse of the Day

> Also that day they offered great sacrifices, and rejoiced, for God had made them rejoice with great joy; the women and the children also rejoiced, so that the joy of Jerusalem was heard afar off.
>
> *Nehemiah 12:43*

Please read the entire Scripture selection in your own Bible and highlight or underline verses that stand out to you before you read the observations and engage the questions below.

In chapter 12, the main message is "Stand and Honor!" Now be honest. How many of you were tempted to skip over this chapter when you saw the long list of names? I've been tempted to do that. In fact, here is a confession: I've preached through the book of Nehemiah before but skipped chapter 12. Yet as I led these journeys through the Bible in the past few years, I realized there are no wasted words in the Bible. The writers of the Bible were not doing what some of us may have done back in college when writing essays that had to be a certain length—just filling space with word salads. Every word of Scripture is preserved for us for a reason, which includes the various rosters of names. In fact, Paul put it this way: "All Scripture is given by inspiration of God, and is profitable for doctrine, for reproof, for correction, for instruction in righteousness, that the man of God may be complete, thoroughly equipped for every good work" (2 Tim. 3:16–17). So, with that understanding, I now approach these differently. I ask the Holy Spirit to open my eyes to see the truth He has for me in these passages that are tempting to go around like a boulder on a trail.

Allow me to set the stage for our study. The walls were rebuilt (chap. 6), the people were spiritually revived (chaps. 7–9), and they began to reform their habits (chaps. 9–10), which by the way is a continual work of God through His Word and the Holy Spirit, as we will see in the remainder of the book of Nehemiah. But at this point, there had been a sea change in the nation; they were back on the right track, moving in the right direction. They were returning to a place of honoring God and the things He did and the things He was doing. Too often, we fail to stop and honor and thank God for what He has done. There is a time for ceremony and celebration, which includes recognition and honor.

Think about it for a moment. Why do you think Hollywood has these elaborate celebrations like the Oscars? I totally disagree with what they celebrate, but they understand that what you celebrate, you'll get more of. We need to celebrate the things of God and honor those who advance the work of God. That is what we have here in the first half of chapter 12—a list of the priests and Levites by name as they returned to Jerusalem from captivity. Look at verse 1: "Now these are the priests and the Levites who came up with Zerubbabel the son of Shealtiel, and Jeshua: Seraiah, Jeremiah, Ezra." I won't repeat all twenty-six of these verses, but I am going to point out what I believe is taking place here.

First of all, they honored the Lord by recognizing those who serve. Were these leaders all perfect? No, I am certain they were not, but whether their contribution was large or small, they were a part of bringing the nation to this point of achievement and accomplishment. Nehemiah recognized that fact, which speaks to his God-honoring humility. He understood that while the Lord used him to accomplish the amazing feat of rebuilding the walls in fifty-two days, there were those who prayed around and over the rubble long before the Lord led him to rebuild it.

Look at verses 10–11: "Jeshua begot Joiakim, Joiakim begot Eliashib, Eliashib begot Joiada, 11 Joiada begot Jonathan, and Jonathan begot Jaddua." Here we have six generations of high priests. After the return from Babylon, the chronology of the Jewish people was kept by the succession of the high priests rather than the kings, as the spiritual leadership defined the nation. The application is straightforward: We should honor the Lord by recognizing those who serve.

Second, they honored the Lord with thanksgiving and celebration. Think about all the preparation, planning, and logistics that would have been involved as you look back over verses 27–31:

Now at the dedication of the wall of Jerusalem they sought out the Levites in all their places, to bring them to Jerusalem to celebrate the dedication with gladness, both with thanksgivings and singing, with cymbals and stringed instruments and harps. And the sons of the singers gathered together from the countryside around Jerusalem, from the villages of the Netophathites, from the house of Gilgal, and from the fields of Geba and Azmaveth; for the singers had built themselves villages all around Jerusalem. Then the priests and Levites purified themselves, and purified the people, the gates, and the wall. So I brought the leaders of Judah up on the wall, and appointed two large thanksgiving choirs. One went to the right hand on the wall toward the Refuse Gate.

Notice how Nehemiah put nearly as much thought into organizing this celebration as he did in organizing the people to build the walls. Read further in verses 38, 40, 43:

> The other thanksgiving choir went the opposite way, and I was behind them with half of the people on the wall, going past the Tower of the Ovens as far as the Broad Wall, . . . So the two thanksgiving choirs stood in the house of God, likewise I and the half of the rulers with me; . . . Also that day they offered great sacrifices, and rejoiced, for God had made them rejoice with great joy; the women and the children also rejoiced, so that the joy of Jerusalem was heard afar off.

So Nehemiah divided the people into two groups. Ezra led one group, followed by singers praising God, followed by the civil leaders, then the priests with trumpets, and then Levites with stringed instruments. The second group headed the other way around the city, meeting the first group in the temple court, where they worshipped God together.

Let's step back and get the full picture of what is going on here. The city was encircled with praise and thanksgiving to God as the walls and the city were dedicated to the Lord. The physical walls of the city had spiritual meaning, so the spiritual leaders led the way in the dedication of the restored city. What a celebration!

And third, they honored God with obedience to His Word. They didn't simply put on a big concert of praise and worship and that was it. It wasn't just a "smoke and light" show. They restarted their daily worship as God had prescribed. Look at verses 44–47:

> And at the same time some were appointed over the rooms of the storehouse for the offerings, the firstfruits, and the

tithes, to gather into them from the fields of the cities the portions specified by the Law for the priests and Levites; for Judah rejoiced over the priests and Levites who ministered. Both the singers and the gatekeepers kept the charge of their God and the charge of the purification, according to the command of David and Solomon his son. For in the days of David and Asaph of old there were chiefs of the singers, and songs of praise and thanksgiving to God. In the days of Zerubbabel and in the days of Nehemiah all Israel gave the portions for the singers and the gatekeepers, a portion for each day. They also consecrated holy things for the Levites, and the Levites consecrated them for the children of Aaron.

Obviously, we no longer bring animals to sacrifice before the Lord. Jesus made Himself a sacrifice once and for all on the cross, and God accepted it as payment for our sins. The proof is in the fact that God raised Him from the dead on the third day. So what sacrifice do we bring to the Lord? We bring the sacrifice of praise and worship. I am reminded of the lyrics from award winning songwriter Matt Redman's worship song "The Heart of Worship." Redman wrote it after his church went through a time of soul-searching with regard to the sincerity of their worship. Their pastor asked them to strip everything down to the basics, no sound system or instruments, and challenged: "When you come through the doors on a Sunday, what are you bringing as your offering to God?" Through that experience, Redman claims they "gained a new perspective that worship is all about Jesus . . . ." Redman wrote the song in his bedroom almost as a cathartic exercise, a confession to the Lord:

When the music fades, all is stripped away, and I simply come / Longing just to bring something that's of worth that will bless your heart . . . . / I'm coming back to the heart of worship, and it's all about You, Jesus.[5]

Honoring God doesn't end with public pronouncements or even celebrations involving worship music. Honoring God continues in the daily, often unseen declarations of obedience to God. A people are not defined by their celebrations of ideals and beliefs but by their daily allegiance and obedience to the foundational truths upon which those beliefs and ideals rest. It is declaring not only with our lips but also with our lives, "It's all about You, Lord."

Questions for Reflection and Discussion

1. Why did the people hold a dedication ceremony?
   a. Completion of the temple
   b. Completion of the royal palace
   c. Completion of the walls around Jerusalem
   d. None of the above

2. How did the people demonstrate their thankfulness to God for His goodness (see v. 43)?

Notes on Today's Bible Reading

_____

_____

_____

_____

_____

_____

— DAY 14 —

Today's Reading: Nehemiah 13

Verse of the Day

[A]nd I came to Jerusalem and discovered the evil that Eliashib had done for Tobiah, in preparing a room for him in the courts of the house of God.

Nehemiah 13:7

Please read the entire Scripture selection in your own Bible and highlight or underline verses that stand out to you before you read the observations and engage the questions below.

Today's churches face many challenges, but I believe one of the most challenging issues is our failure to exercise discipline. More often than not, we avoid confrontation out of fear of offending someone or hurting their feelings. Instead, we need to learn to confront what is contrary to God's Word. In the final chapter of Nehemiah, we learn Nehemiah dished out some discipline, and it was based on Scripture.

Look back at verses 1–3: "On that day they read from the Book of Moses in the hearing of the people, and in it was found written that no Ammonite or Moabite should ever come into the assembly of God, because they had not met the children of Israel with bread and water, but hired Balaam against them to curse them. However, our God turned the curse into a blessing. So it was, when they had heard the Law, that they separated all the mixed multitude from Israel."

We have learned the Word of God is the authoritative standard, but when a culture moves away from it, applying that standard may lead to confrontation. This is what Nehemiah faced. Because long ago the people had forgotten God's Word, they engaged in mixed marriages. So Nehemiah confronted it based on the Word of God. It's not there only to study. It's there to follow, order our lives by, and it is for correction. That's the confrontation, for instruction in righteousness (also see 2 Tim. 3:16).

First, notice what was happening in the temple in verses 4–7:

> Now before this, Eliashib the priest, having authority over the storerooms of the house of our God, was allied with Tobiah. And he had prepared for him a large room, where previously they had stored the grain offerings, the frankincense, the articles, the tithes of grain, the new wine and oil, which were commanded to be given to the Levites and singers and gatekeepers, and the offerings for the priests. But during all this I was not in Jerusalem, for in the thirty-second year of Artaxerxes king of Babylon I had returned to the king. Then after certain days I obtained leave from the king, and I came to Jerusalem and discovered the evil that Eliashib had done for Tobiah, in preparing a room for him in the courts of the house of God.

How did Nehemiah respond to this clear biblical violation? Did he say, "And it grieved me bitterly, so I went home and I stewed about it"? No. He said, "And it grieved me bitterly; therefore I threw all the household goods of Tobiah out of the room. Then I commanded them to cleanse the rooms; and I brought back into them the articles of the house of God, with the grain offering and the frankincense." Wow. He was a mean guy. Some might think this. But no, he took action because he was grieved about the violation of God's standard.

This incident reminds me of the action taken by the Lord Jesus in Matthew 21:12–13: "Then Jesus went into the temple of God and drove out all of those who bought and sold in the temple and overturned the tables of the money changers and the seats of those who sold doves. And he said to them, it is written, my house shall be called a house of prayer. But you have made it a den of thieves." You mean Jesus did that? He turned over tables. He did. He confronted that which violated the Word of God.

Here's something I want you to understand. If your worship of the Lord is compromised, your relationship with others will be corrupted. The people compromised the standard of God both in Nehemiah's day—what was supposed to be for offerings to God was set up as an apartment for His enemy—and in Jesus's day— a house of prayer was turned into a place where marketers and merchants took advantage of people. And so, compromising worship of the Lord can corrupt relationships with others.

We must understand something else about confrontation. It's not about our views. It's not about our feelings or our emotions. We don't confront people because they really made us mad. That's not godly confrontation. It's not even about the fact that we were offended. That does not matter a hill of beans. What matters is the standard of God. If that standard is violated, a leader must confront the situation and the person or persons involved. We confront it with love and compassion and mercy, but it must be confronted: "Preach the word! Be ready in season and out of season. Convince, rebuke, exhort with all longsuffering and teaching" (2 Tim. 4:2).

Again, the responsibilities that fall upon a leader require confronting that which violates God's standard. If we sweep it under the rug, if we ignore it, it will only become more profound and pronounced. And it will become contagious. You may recall Paul urged redemptive confrontation in his letters to churches, especially to the Corinthians, where he instructed them to break fellowship with those who refused to abide by the standard of God. Today, however, it seems we feel like offending someone is a greater sin than offending God.

If you're going to be a leader and maintain fellowship with God and have the power of the Holy Spirit in your life, you have to realize leadership may cause you to lose friends and fellowship with individuals. I am not saying we recklessly use confrontation as leaders. It is a last resort. But there are times when those who are openly violating the Word of God must be confronted—lovingly, with the hope and desire they will repent and return to that standard. But it must be done, and we must get back to church discipline.

I'll close with what is really the overarching truth of this study of leadership: Great leaders don't set out to be leaders. They set out to make a difference. And inevitably, others will follow them in the pursuit of that goal. Remember, it's about the goal, not the role. Don't seek to be a leader. Seek to please God and to serve Him in an area of need.

Nehemiah wasn't thinking, *How can I add this to my résumé? I want to build a résumé, and how can I get on the cover of* Time *magazine?* No. Remember, it goes back to compassion. His brother sent a message that the city was in ruins and people were disheartened and discouraged. So by compassion, Nehemiah began to pray, showing humility as he prayed and he fasted, and he began to plan. He practiced the traits of a godly leader. God moves leaders to meet needs that will glorify Him, and He called on Nehemiah to rebuild a nation.

As we conclude this study, I encourage you to take time to reflect on that. Think through these characteristics, the traits that Nehemiah had. Of those, what are the top three you need to strengthen in your life? Pray and ask God to show you. Maybe it's reading from some solid, biblical authors on the issue. Maybe it's as simple as going a little deeper in the Word. Ask the Holy Spirit to show you. But if you're going to lead, at any level, you should work on developing these godly traits so that God can use you to make a difference for His kingdom. Perhaps if enough of us will step up and step out, God will use us to rebuild our broken nation. May God bless you as you serve Him!

Questions for Reflection and Discussion

1. Upon returning to Jerusalem a decade after having resumed his duties in the Persian court as cupbearer, what disturbing developments did Nehemiah find and what did he do about it?
   a. Threw out Tobiah, their adversary, and all his stuff from the temple
   b. Called out the leaders for failing to keep their commitment to the Levites
   c. Pointed out God's law to those profaning the Sabbath
   d. Punched out some of the men who had intermarried with pagans
   e. All of the above

2. What was Nehemiah's final prayer (v. 38)?

Notes on Today's Bible Reading

_____

_____

_____

_____

Appendix 1:

Stand on the Word Bible Reading Plan

Visit frc.org/Bible for our chronological journey through the Bible that we call "Stand on the Word." We encourage you to spend time reading and studying the Bible because it is literally "God-breathed" (2 Tim. 3:16); it is God's very words to us. The Bible answers the big questions, such as, Why am I here? Where did I come from? Where am I going (life after death)? If God is good, why does evil and suffering exist? The Bible not only answers these big questions; it offers practical advice in areas such as, How can I deal with feelings of fear or anger or guilt? How can I forgive when I cannot forget? What should I look for in a spouse? How can I have a successful marriage? How can I be a good parent? What is my spiritual gift and place in the church? What is my stewardship responsibility as a citizen? We learned the verse in Bible School, "Your word is a lamp to my feet and a light to my path" (Ps. 119:105). God's Word shows us the way forward in any area of life and on every question we face.

The Stand on the Word Bible Reading Plan takes us through the Bible chronologically. In other words, each reading takes you through the Bible as events occurred in history as far as it is possible. Here is how it works for our family. At the same time each morning, whether I am at home, in Washington, or some foreign country, I send my wife and children a morning greeting along with a reminder of the passage for the day. The text includes two questions related to the reading. The questions are designed to help in content retention, serve as an accountability tool, and provide for discussion.

The two-year plan does not have a Sunday passage. Instead, it provides an outline for a family discussion that can be done on Sunday afternoon or evening each week. The weekly discussion time begins with a spiritual leader asking each person individually for one or two insights or truths they gained from their reading during the week. After everyone else shares, you can then lead a short discussion based upon one of the passages that you read in the week just completed. It is also a time for them to ask questions.

By the way, you don't have to have all the answers. If you don't know, tell them so, then talk to your pastor or other trusted person with Bible knowledge. If your children start asking questions, that suggests they are thinking about what they are reading.

Reading God's Word will help you establish a fruitful walk with the God who made you and loves you. Whether you are single or married, this plan will enable you to lead your friends and family in daily reading God's Word. The added benefit is that you will all be reading the same text together. It will amaze you to see how God speaks sometimes in the same ways and at other times in different ways to each of you. Being on this journey together will build a spiritual synergy, a deep bond and sense of unity and purpose like nothing else! Use it to impart the Word of life.

Appendix 2:
Prayer: Talking with God

Most Americans say they pray. But not as many pray the way Jesus did, the way He taught His disciples to pray. Fewer, still, really know the power in prayer God gave us to impact our families, communities, nation, and world. Prayer is our lifeline to God, our means of communicating with our heavenly Father. It develops our relationship—our friendship, fellowship, and intimacy with Him. In prayer we experience God and are "filled with the Spirit" (see Eph. 5:18–21). God uses the prayers of faithful men, women, boys, and girls to heal broken lives and strengthen families, churches, communities, and even nations. He uses our prayers to advance his Kingdom on earth (Daniel 9; Acts 4:36). He wants to use all believers!

The Essence of Prayer

Prayer is simply talking with God—about anything and everything. He is our Maker, Father, Savior, Provider, and Counselor; our Master, Healer, Guide, and Friend. Christ died for our sins and rose from the dead to sit at the right hand of God the Father, where He is praying for us *right now* (Heb. 10:12). His Spirit now lives within us and helps us to pray (1 John 4:16).

The Priority of Prayer

Jesus spent time alone with God regularly drawing strength from the Father and seeking His will for every decision (Luke 6:12–13; 22:39–44). His disciples asked Jesus to teach them how to pray (Luke 11:1–13). The apostles knew that prayer and obedience were the keys to Christ's life and ministry and were determined to follow His example: "[W]e will devote ourselves to prayer and to the ministry of the word" (Acts 6:4). Too few American men pray today, even pastors and leaders! Yet strong praying men are the norm in Scripture. Our families, churches, and nation need men who will make prayer a priority today! (1 Tim. 2:8).

The Practice of Prayer

Scripture teaches, "Pray continually!" (1 Thess. 5:17); "Pray always" (Eph. 6:18); "Always pray and do not give up" (Luke 18:1). Below are some helps to get you started. No one can beat the Lord's Prayer. It is an outline of key themes to guide our prayer lives: "Our Father in heaven, hallowed be your name. Your kingdom come, your will be done, on earth as it is in heaven. Give us this day our daily bread, and forgive us our debts, as we also have forgiven our debtors. And lead us not into temptation, but deliver us from evil" (Matt. 6:9–13).

In the book of Psalms and throughout Scripture, God has sprinkled prayers/patterns for us to learn from. Here is a simple, popular acronym to help jog our memories:

P-R-A-Y:

- *Praise:* Our Father which art in heaven, hallowed be thy name.
- *Repent:* And forgive us our debts, as we forgive our debtors.

- *Ask:* Give us this day our daily bread. And forgive us our debts, as we forgive our debtors. And lead us not into temptation but deliver us from evil.
- *Yield:* Thy kingdom come. Thy will be done in earth, as it is in heaven.

Praying through Scripture

God also talks to us. The Bible is His Word (2 Tim. 2:15; 3:16). Bible in hand, we should pray God's promises back to Him and claim them for our families, our work, our finances, and our nation (1 Tim. 2:1–8; 1 John 5:14–15).

Scriptures to Pray as a Man: Joshua 1:8; 1 Timothy 3:1–15; 1 Chronicles 12:32; 1 Timothy 6:1–12; 1 Corinthians 16:13; Romans 12:1–21; Micah 6:8; John 4:24; Acts 2:38: 1 Kings 2:2; Ephesians 5:25–28; Genesis 2:24; 1 Peter 3:7; Ephesians 4:26–27; Matthew 5:32; Proverbs 5:19; 1 Corinthians 6:18; Deuteronomy 4:8–10; 11:18–21; Exodus 34:5–8; Psalm 127:3–5; Matthew 7:11; Ephesians 6:4; Proverbs 22:6; Luke 11:11–12; Hebrews 12:5–7

Scriptures to Pray as a Woman: Matthew 22:36–40; Proverbs 31:30; 1 Peter 3:1–3; Ephesians 5:26; Ephesians 4:15, 29; 1 Timothy 3:11; Ephesians 5:22, 24; 1 Peter 3:1–2; Philippians 4:10–13; Philippians 2:3–4; Proverbs 31:12; 1 Corinthians 7:34; Titus 2:3–4; Titus 2:4–5; James 1:19; Ephesians 4:32; 1 Corinthians 7:1–5; Luke 2:37; Colossians 4:2; Proverbs 31:27; 1 Timothy 5:14; 1 Timothy 5:14

Scriptures to Pray for Your Children: Matthew 22:36–40; 2 Timothy 3:15; Psalm 97:10, 38:18; Proverbs 8:13; John 17:15, 10:10; Romans 12:9; Psalm 119:71; Hebrews 12:5–6; Daniel 1:17, 20; Proverbs 1:4; James 1:5; Romans 13:1; Ephesians 6:1–3; Hebrews 13:17; Proverbs 1:10–16; 13:20; 2 Corinthians 6:14–17; Deuteronomy 6; 1 Corinthians 6:18–20; Acts 24:16; 1 Timothy 1:19,

4:1–2; Titus 1:15–16; Psalm 23:4; Deuteronomy 10:12; Matthew 28:18–20; Ephesians 1:3, 4:29; Ephesians 1:16–19; Philippians 1:11; Colossians 1:9; Philippians 1:9–10

Developing Personal Prayer Habits

Rise early each day to pray with opened Bible. Daniel prayed three times daily. Pray whenever you can: as you drive, with your wife, with your children at dinner and before bedtime. You cannot pray too much!

Praying Together with Others

Pray with your spouse regularly. Make time for family prayer. Be part of your church prayer meeting or group. Christ said, "My house shall be called a house of prayer" (Matt. 21:13). The apostle Paul instructed Pastor Timothy to make prayer the first order of the church, saying prayer is key to peace in the nation (1 Tim. 2:1–8). There is nothing like a Spirit-led prayer meeting with people who love the Lord! Praying women have been standing in the prayer gap for decades. Every man must set his heart to become a praying man, lead his family in prayer, and be a strong contributor to the corporate prayer life of his church. We must be leaders in praying for our morally and spiritually troubled, divided nation—and for our national leaders. American Christians simply must respond to God's promise: "If My people who are called by My name will humble themselves, and pray and seek My face, and turn from their wicked ways, then I will hear from heaven, and will forgive their sin and heal their land" (2 Chron. 7:14).

Prayer As Warfare

Jesus described the enemy, the devil, as a thief whose mission is to "steal, kill and destroy" (John 10:10). Demonic forces are at war against everything good in you, your family, your church, your community, America, and every nation (Ephesians 6:10–20).

The devil and his minions are out to thwart the kingdom of God and eliminate righteousness wherever he can. He hates God and hates people and will use spiritually ignorant and deceived men, women, boys, and girls to do his bidding. Men of God today, like the sons of Issachar in ancient Israel, need to understand the times and know what the church and our nation must do (1 Chron. 12:32). We must pull down Satan's strongholds, wrestle for our families, and use Spirit-led prayer and wisdom to help guide our churches and communities to prevail against the evil onslaught against us (2 Cor. 10:3–5). This is the war of the ages, and it is real.

Finally, Determine to Become a Person of Prayer

No matter how long you have been a Christian and may have neglected prayer up until now, you can become a person of prayer starting today. If you have missed the mark, it is not too late. Call upon the Lord, ask for His help, and proceed with His guidance. O Lord, make me a praying person; make me a prayer warrior! In Jesus's name, amen!